HOGGWASH

The Callaghan and Rosenblatt
Epistolary Convergence

HOGGWASH

The Callaghan and Rosenblatt Epistolary Convergence

Introduction by Catherine Owen

EXILE
editions

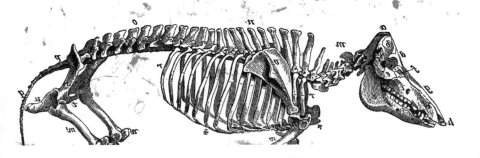

Library and Archives Canada Cataloguing in Publication

Callaghan, Barry, 1937-, author
Hoggwash : the Callaghan and Rosenblatt epistolary convergence / BarryCallaghan,
Joe Rosenblatt ; introduction by Catherine Owen.

Includes index.
Monograph includes artwork by both Barry Callaghan and Joe Rosenblatt.
Issued in print and electronic formats.
ISBN 978-1-55096-509-4 (paperback).--ISBN 978-1-55096-514-8 (epub).--
ISBN 978-1-55096-521-6 (mobi).--ISBN 978-1-55096-531-5 (pdf)

1. Callaghan, Barry, 1937- --Correspondence. 2. Rosenblatt, Joe, 1933-
--Correspondence. 3. Callaghan, Barry, 1937-. 4. Rosenblatt, Joe, 1933-.
5. Authors, Canadian (English)--20th century--Correspondence.
I. Rosenblatt, Joe, 1933-, author II. Title.

PS8555.A49Z545 2016   C811'.54   C2015-906961-0
                                       C2015-906962-9

Text Design and Interior Composition by Mishi Uroboros
Typeset in Big Caslon font at Moons of Jupiter Studios

Published by Exile Editions Ltd ~ www.ExileEditions.com
144483 Southgate Road 14 – GD, Holstein, Ontario, N0G 2A0
Printed and Bound in Canada in 2015, by Marquis

We gratefully acknowledge, for their support toward our publishing activities,
the Canada Council for the Arts, the Government of Canada through
the Canada Book Fund (CBF), the Ontario Arts Council,
and the Ontario Media Development Corporation.

Canadian Sales: The Canadian Manda Group, 664 Annette Street,
Toronto ON M6S 2C8 www.mandagroup.com 416 516 0911

North American and international distribution, and U.S. sales:
Independent Publishers Group, 814 North Franklin Street,
Chicago IL 60610 www.ipgbook.com toll free: 1 800 888 4741

for Vera Frenkel

CONTENTS

CASTING PEARLS BEFORE A PIG
An Epistolary Exchange between Hogg and the Bee-Man
by Catherine Owen

Joe Rosenblatt and Barry Callaghan have been scribing, tippling, combative, ecstatic compadres for over 40 years. Otherwise utterly divergent personalities, with Callaghan, among an array of chapeaus, donning the roles of professor, man of belles lettres and publisher while Rosenblatt choosing, with his oft-repeated allegiance to the buzzers, chirpers and purrers of the world, to remain aloof from the human masses, preferring to daub and scrawl in more private realms. They remain conjoined amicably across Canadian distances by their shared dedication to the word. *Hoggwash: The Callaghan and Rosenblatt Epistolary Convergence* is a tribute to their enduring friendship.

In 1978, Callaghan's *The Hogg Poems and Drawings* was published – a poetic sequence that delves into the protagonist's semi-religious quest to Jerusalem, a sojourn that enables him to seek release from the stultifying institutions and denizens of Hogtown, aka Toronto. Post-pilgrimage, recharged by the passionate absurdities and historical engagements of the Old World, Hogg further routs up his roots through a descent into his hometown's subway system. After three further instantiations of Hogg, a final volume of Hogg's pronouncements. This time, missives from a psychic gulag in Russia, *Seven Last Words*, appeared in 2001. Alternately paranoid and perverse, Hogg relentlessly sounds a rebellious *cri de coeur* that pledges fidelity to the artistic vision over and above any constraining forces.

The *Hoggwash* interchange commences with a delirious interview of sorts between Barry and Joe, a framing device that serves to paint Rosenblatt as the numinous bee-man he is, voyeur of poetic pollinations, blatantly leering at the spectacle too of baboons, bats, cats and other temptresses in a "great striptease of [a] garden." Thus forewarned of the bards' penchants, the reader is treated to the first missive in this rumpus of a discourse, this eventual clashing and conjoining of literary titans over such bugaboos as Heidegger, Catholicism, fascism, sex, art, mothers, and whether one can express feelings of intimacy for mere trout. JR opens his parry with a concern for his long-term friend's alter ego, the bombastic, libidinously inclined and apparently conflicted Hogg, a partitioned Catholic grossly divided, according to Rosenblatt, betwixt the sacred and profane, half-driven to sexual excesses when he isn't chanting *Te Deum laudamus te Dominum confitemur te aeternum Patrem omnis terra venerator* on his knees, caught as he is between the Kama Sutra and the Stations of the Cross. Callaghan, while admitting to a rift between himself, a "gadabout and rounder" with no "gift for philosophical musing" and the loquacious Hogg with his yen for aletheia despite his recurrent neuroses, recoils from Rosenblatt's retentive perplexity in the face of his anti-Doppelganger's apparently binaric collisions of spirit and flesh. And so it goes. A jab by Rosenblatt; a left hook by Hogg. Yet this pugilism is no simple spectacle, no base jousting of the loggerheads persuasion. Deep and rupturing issues are at stake here. As Rosenblatt notes, these letters not only take up the rapture and DNA of poetry but its relevance in a material world driven by genocide and war. Thus, one of the most painful clashes is Rosenblatt's proximity in a familial sense to Hitler's genocidal wreckages as contrasted with Hogg's ability to continue to venerate artists who spoke in support of the Third Reich, determined as he is to slash the Siamese twins of politics and art down their cleaved middle. While Hogg can pontificate about Pound, for instance, stating that he will not "cast him out like a devil" but take what he "can learn from his great gifts – his lucid line, his musical dexterity – and turn those gifts against the fascist ideas he espoused," Rosenblatt refutes Hogg's ability to separate the creation from the human, pronouncing fiercely: "The Holocaust still resonates with me, and I can't waft it away like so much bog vapour." With other men, artists or no, such differences might lead to silence, violent dissention, even hatred, but Rosenblatt and Callaghan's writerly personas are capable of o'er leaping any divide through their common devotion to the sanctity of the word. Hogg propounds: "The first casualty of war is language," a battle neither bard is willing to bloody himself in, as the stakes are too great: art before politics, always, though the latter is implicated at a nearly somatic level in the former.

To the fascination of these crusty correspondents' dialectic on a spectrum of issues, add the pique inherent in being let into the cortextual sanctum of their self-perceptions, and the way they thus view each other's quirks and quarks of personality. While Hogg sees his persona as being a finely fused entity of only superficially dichotomous paradigms (lusty and pious for instance), Rosenblatt openly states his bafflement, gasping how "unsettled and confused" he is by Hogg's rampant "juxtapositions" between, in Yeatsian terms, the "heavenly mansion and the place of excrement," and judging him, at least initially, as a "divided Hogg." Similarly, Rosenblatt, steeped in his nirvana of inter species sonnet-spasmodic hotness, his straight-laced puritanical persona shrinking from the word "cunt," dubs himself a rational, clear-eyed adherent of "the transcendent ingurgitating power of the Stoma," and yet still rails against Hogg's pronouncement that there is no "intimacy" in his poetry and that he is affected by a rank prudery, calling out "Mother, Mother" every time Hogg ruts out the rallying cry of "Fuck!"

The two personas' grating principles are further embodied by the inclusion of their drawings. Hogg's are ripe and terrifying, their Blakean energies pulsating within vigorous strokes and delineations of nightmarish, yet eroticized, proportions; Rosenblatt's sketching out the cat-eat-bird world in a more dreamily detached assemblage of images. Their excerpted poems too underscore their divergences. Rosenblatt has a dying bumblebee fall "on his pollen-laden elbows/in Momma's tabernacle" while Hogg envisages the Almighty giving fellatio to a minaret, "that stone shaft into/the mouth of god." The contrasts in their poetic, artistic and personal relationship to the universe are often startling, arousing, discombobulating.

And yet, nothing has ruptured their capacity for intricately argued discourse and the freedom of mind this entails. The reader comes to understand how implicated he or she has been in this engaging repartee, alternately taking sides, at times resisting both points of view, sometimes even agreeing with each, suddenly realizing there are sly jokes running throughout (Hogg's disparaging views of Callaghan as a man who lacks intellectual weight). Most crucially, this risky "convergence" highlights – by being quite its opposite – the awful timorousness that exists in Canadian letters today. How many poets would beg to disagree on so many key concerns and remain amiable, even wholly supportive of each other's art? How many would skirmish in such watery dark realms and yet surface time and again to a land of *pax*? Though Callaghan deigns at the end to inform Joe that his cherished "fondling and stroking of a fish" is "repulsive" to him, still the missives conclude with his finny compatriot thanking him for his honesty and admitting that "it was a pleasure carrying on an epistolary discourse." It is this kind of rambunctious, irreverent and invigorating descant that is frequently missing from our literary bullring. Callaghan acknowledges that this exchange reveals the miracle of a friendship that has lasted and lasted between a most unlikely pair over great distances, and that when these erudite challenges were offered (if not hurled), they were done so knowing no offence would be taken, but would only result in an increase of companionship and mutual admiration. *Hoggwash* therefore exists to remind us there are other ways of holding intellectual and artistic relationships on this fraught planet than those that solely fawn, those that mainly fear.

THE CONVERSATION

Barry Callaghan and Joe Rosenblatt

When things go wrong and will not come right,
Though you do the best you can,
When life looks black as the hour of night,
A PINT OF PLAIN IS YOUR ONLY MAN.

—FLANN O'BRIEN, *At Swim-Two-Birds*

BARRY CALLAGHAN

On a given day, if Joe Rosenblatt finds that his *brain is pregnant with murder* and if he *sniffs an evil truffle rotting in the black earth*, he is liable to turn as mean as Ambrose Bierce, that misanthropic storyteller whose idea of whimsicality almost always had a homicidal edge ("early one June morning in 1872 I murdered my father – an act which made a deep impression on me at the time"), a writer whose characters never seemed to suffer as men and women but to suffer more like caged animals.

However, should Rosenblatt find that he is able to relax a little and should he realize that he is welcome to let his *matured bones* return home

> *to sit in the old wicker chair*
> *…on a mystery drive*
> *down a country road with pebbles flying*

then he will hear not just Bierce in himself but echoes of the visionary Hart Crane, who wrote:

> *Sing!*
> *…the imponderable dinosaur*
> *sinks slow,*
> *the mammoth saurian*
> *ghoul…*

Rosenblatt will then lie down *dazzled at the round door* of his sweet serpent, murmuring:

> *Welcome to my parlour, diaphanous lady,*
> *we've met before in another room*
> *where silence nudged each corner cool & shady*
> *& both our moons suffused as in a marbled tomb.*

It is entrancing to think of Joe Rosenblatt having been bred by Hart Crane out of Ambrose Bierce...and to then find him sitting here in a darkened room, sitting so deep in the shadows that he can hardly be seen, talking about how he has actually watched *holes walk off a golf course*, has actually seen several *exterminators grunting like warty hogs* get ready to *ventilate his body* with pitchforks...and so, here in this darkened room I said to my friend Joe as casually as I could, "You seem to me to be a blue angel, always in a delirium of poems and in this delirium you are, over and over again, *born like death, with burning branches growing*...You are always, in short, in danger...?"

I would say you were getting very close to the truth there. I always feel that I am suffocated – in cells, cages, nets, traps. When I worked for the railway for about six and a half years, it was a job that provided plenty of security, but it was a mindless back-breaking type of toil. I thought I'd never be liberated. I couldn't even get laid off, I had so much seniority. You might say it was a cage. Well lit. But a cage. It isn't just a question of employment: it's also the relationships I have had with women, which were cages, or traps.

B.C.

Are people moving in on you all the time, surrounding you, coming at you with whatever weapons they call their own?

J.R.

I've seen violence in my time, the cold blue eyes of hungry killers. I've been involved in real street fighting and I've had to battle Nazis and types like that, you know. So I've seen violence, family corpses sitting at their morning table.

B.C.

Would it be accurate to say that there's a new romance attached to extremes of violence and that you're a very romantic poet?

J.R.

It would be more accurate to say that in my *zoos of incongruity* I'm a disillusioned romantic:

> *& she did tricks*
> *for sightless psyches: Braille striptease*
> *in a blind pig where sewer gas burns away*
> *& all illusions flow into one Nile.*

B.C.

A romantic who also happens to hang out at the baboon cage in Vancouver's Stanley Park?

J.R.

I used to go every day because I sort of identified with the incarcerated individual, this baboon. I keep calling him a person. You will have to excuse me because, for one thing, the people outside his living room, or his cage, reinforced their egos by saying he looked stupid. Look at the red, white, and blue stigmata on his nose, look how dumb he is, he's begging, he's humbling himself. For me this creature became a symbol of the crucified animal.

B.C.

Do you think men transfer a visceral need for violence, their awareness of their own stupidity, to the baboon?

J.R.

Yes, yes, I've seen this on a number of occasions. The baboon becomes a neurotic because – and I have in mind one given case

– there is no psychedelic female around. No sexual strokes. You know how we put people in prisons in this country. Our outcasts, our outsiders. The baboon was a political prisoner of Man. He was constantly persecuted, reduced to being a beggar, a stomach, fortifying the Stoma Principle. But it was still quite beautiful for me to watch the poetry of his hands, the mime of his fingers, his very small infant fingers. And he moved them with a watchmaker's precision. That was poetry in motion. He was the only hip poet in Vancouver, a mandrill baboon, you could watch how

> *his hazelnut eyes explored the landscape*
> *old men totter from park benches*
> *to chew theology with a primate*
> *who urges them to kiss his hot plate bottom.*
> *The joker opens wide his canine mouth*
> *declaring twins, his sabre teeth.*

B.C.

What about bats? What did you find so interesting about our nocturnal creature, the bat?

J.R.

I happened to be wandering through the aviary, where all the bats are housed in a cage – like a shop window, you look inside, and these fruit bats, with their enormous leathern wings and fascinating metacarpus structure – every one of them quite hideous looking if you base your view of beauty and goodness on Christian superstition. Here is the evil bat who lives in underground caves. I kept looking at this thing. I was quite amazed by it. I had this obsession, and after a while – as I kept looking at it – the bat finally opened its wings to me and there was the most beautiful body, a rodent body with beautiful ears and very sensitive eyes. My prejudice was exorcised. I then got involved with the whole mythology, the superstitions about the bat, to the point where I was studying acoustics, echo location, sonar, decibels. I got involved in the whole cosmology, as I had done with the baboon. But the bat to me was an even more gripping symbol of Darkness, this creature of the subconscious, our subconscious.

B.C.

In the darkness, you found the real presence of beauty?

J.R.

Right.

In this Martian landscape
I realize there is no sex life after
     death.
E.S.P. raincoats grapple ceiling with
     cargo hook fingers
As they leap, they dream, dream of fruit
     bat salads
ambrosia and porny: nectarines of
     virgin bats
Sweeter than rotting peaches, apples,
     Plus...

B.C.

A beauty alien to men. And to women.

J.R.

At least, alien in their waking hours. But in the nighttime...
that's when

The zombie yawns...yawns...yawns...
He's scratching himself again.
(O pity the fleas in his carpet.)
Take away the bastard's wings
and he'd swing with mini Red Riding Hood
for something perversely human is happening:
peeking thru his death robe
a wee pink-nippled carrot?

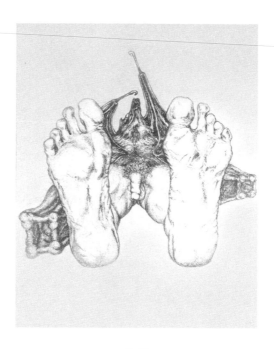

B.C.

And I hear tell you spent a good deal of time that summer on your stomach, eyeballing bees.

J.R.

Yes, yes, a strange type of voyeurism isn't it? I am the chief voyeur in my own garden of moments. It all started in Kitsilano in Vancouver when I happened to walk down to the beach and there was a lovely park, it was down below 1st Avenue, maybe it was Jericho Beach. There was this big buzzing, hovering bumblebee, it just suddenly dived into the hollow of this flower and I didn't think very much of it at first, but then it persistently and very forcefully went into another flower and there was the whole, you know, male and female principle working itself out in a simple, dialectical way.

And so I let that go for a time, and took a few mental notes – I never carry a pencil with me, I always have to remember whatever I damn well see – but subsequently, as I became more and more obsessed with the bumblebee, I made all kinds of notes at home. Then when I came back to the garden I looked at every aspect of the bumblebee and found out that on the rear legs there are little grooves or bread baskets that are perfectly meant for what the bumblebee does: he brushes back all the pollen – he's a six-legged creature – and stores it in these bread baskets. You start looking at the lumps of pollen on the rear legs and you realize you're invading the privacy of the bee while he's going around trying to bring home the powder to the Queen:

> *Bees are truck drivers of the sky*
> *who burrow into diners of flowers*
> *to be fed therein, & overhauled.*
> *"I'll try another flower," thinks the honeybee,*
> *"taste so goddam delicious, this flower*
> *ummmmm…such O dour, & colour."*
> *Buzzzzzzzzzzzzzzzzzzzzzzzzz flip flip…*
> *Pregnant with proletarian bug song*
> *they carry their freight of pollen groceries*
> *home to Momma – the boss queen!*

B.C.

About your bees, about the bats, about the "municipal birds with varicose veins," there's a human sexual inference: are you a Henry Miller with bat wings? The bats and the bees love one another, they cheat on one another, they're crazy for pistils and pudenda, unfettered, free to let it all be, because you say, "for bats there are no babysitters."

J.R.

I gotta sidetrack you there, because when I first came across the bumblebee I thought, there it is, forcing its way into the petals, into the church of the flower, and I also thought – listening to them as they penetrated, I thought the poetic line that I could get from that sound was a way for me to break out of that most hidebound of all traps, that most awful cage: iambic pentameter. I was seeing that the bees going down into the flowers made them very male, but it turns out (and ain't this the truth about life), all these workers are sterile females. I envisioned butch bees with their tubes tied driving their ten-, twelve-wheelers down the road…power drivers:

Bees are truck drivers of the sky
who buzz into diners
demanding lobotomies for breakfast:
waitresses of flies scatter
before the maniacs of proletarians—
each blossom becomes a delicious body house
for diesel dancers in the atmosphere

$$Bzzzzzzzzzzzzzzzzzzzzzzzzzzz$$
Zzzzzzzzzzzzzzzzzzzzzzzzzzzzzzzzzzzzzzzzzzzzzzzzzzzz
Zzzzzzzzz
   blip! blip! blip! blip! blip! blip! blip! blip! zzzzzzzzzz
zzzzzzzzz ssssssssssssssss zzzzzz blipblipblip   zzzzzzzzz

                             z
                            z
                          z
                        z
                     z
                  z

bizzzzzzzzzzzzzzzzzzzzzzzzzzzzzzzzzzzzzzzzzzzzzzzzzzzzz
zzzzzzzzzzzzzzzzzzzzzzzzzzzzzzzzzzzzzzzzzzzzzzzzzzzzzz
zzzzzzzzzzzzzzzzzzzzzzzzz   b1zzzzzzzzzzzzzzzzzzzzzzz
zzzzzzzzzzzzzzzzzzzzzzzz   b1zzzzzzzzzzzzzzzzzzzzzzzz
buzzzzzzzzzzzzzzzzzzzzzz   zzzzzzzzz   zzzzzzzzzzzzz

b1zzzzz zzzzzz zzzzzzz   zzzzz   zzzzzzzzzzz

z
z   z
z
z   z
z
z   z
z
z   z
z

zzzzzzzzzzzzzzzzzzzzzzzzzzzzzzzzzzzzzzzzzzzzzzzzzzzzzzzz
Bizzzzzzzzzzzzzzzzzzzzzzzzzzzzzzz

z
z   z
z
z   z
z
z   z
z
z   z
b
e
z
z
z
z
z
z
z
z
z
z

z   bees are, animal

z	*bees are, animal*
z	*bees are, animal*
	bees are, animal
z	*bees are, animal*
z	*bees are, animal*
z	*bees are, animal*
z	*bees are, animal*
z	*bees are, animal*
z	*bees are, animal*
z	*bees are, animal*
z	*bees are, animal*
z	*bees are, animal*
z	*bees are, animal*
z	*bees are, animal*
z	*bees are, animal*
z	*bees are, animal*
z	*bees are, animal*
z	*bees are, animal*
	bees
	bees
	bees
	bees
	bees
	bees
	bees
	bees

B.C.

Joe, goddam ZZZZZ, you've got me doing it. You've got this kind of incantation going on. Bees are, bees are, bees are... you're a bee dreamer, a louche lothario among bats. ZZZZZZZ, you're the bees' knees.

J.R.

Yes, yes, you sound like you're losing your mind, but what you say is partially true. Yes, I have from time to time tried to find "a diaphanous lady" with whom I could form a relationship. Now, I've written the odd human poem. I don't often do that. I'm too far alienated, I just don't find humans as interesting, dammit, as bees, baboons, serpents and bats unburdening their penises in the cave.

B.C.

But I hear from your *invisible chauffeur*, your spirit who *keeps the pebbles flying*, that a love poem has slipped from out of your sleeve:

J.R.

Well, not exactly out of my sleeve, it's my love poem for my wife, Faye, but yes:

Love is deep as a freshly killed bird
stroked by scimitars, measured by a whisker,
On everybody's doormat
there is a sleeping bird.

We want to forget
still we feel the warmth. It hops on one leg
or hangs on a branch
with a broken wing.

In this
land of eelgrass
and ice drifts and snow, how does a
man live through an endless winter of endless
nights, and how does he stay sane while sitting
squat hour after hour by a seal hole in the ice,
waiting for the snout of the seal, for the one heave
of the harpoon that he can make into the dark
water, and then groping in the water under the ice,
feeling for the dead bulk of the seal body, hauling
it home, the moment of triumph as brief as the
arctic summer in which the sun shines
all night, exhausting itself in a last
lunge against the dark
and then the cleft
of light
closes

—Hogg

THE CONVERGENCES

Epistles between Joe Rosenblatt and Hogg

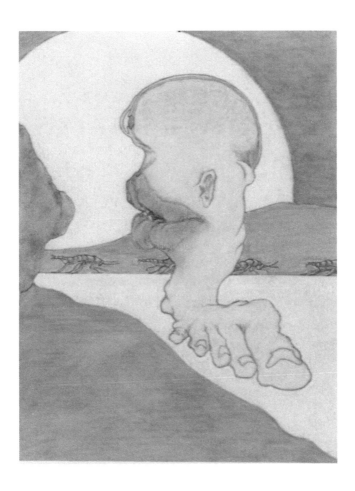

August 21

Mr. —— Hogg
69 Ophidian Crescent
Mimico, Ontario

Dear Mr. Hogg,

I enjoyed our conversation on the phone last week. I want to thank you for agreeing to answer my questions relating to *Hogg*, your long poem. Before I begin with my queries, I wish to acknowledge my gratitude to my friend and publisher, Barry Callaghan, for arranging our discourse. Analyzing your bristly masterwork proved an adventure for me. At times, lured by flickering *idée fixes*, I found myself sinking up to my sloped shoulder in the ooze of theological quicksand.

My work, *The Lunatic Muse*, began its life as *The Lunatic Muse: The Mythopoeic in Canadian Poetry*, a paper delivered to Italian scholars at the University of Bologna. I then attempted to develop that amusing screed; I began to reflect on "the fine madness" of some iconic Canadian poets who had befriended and mentored me in the early '60s. I began to dwell on the mystical components in the poetry of Gwendolyn MacEwen, Milton Acorn – and having read Hogg in the mid-'70s, and knowing that it had struck a chord with MacEwen – decided that your lively muse was ripe for the probing.

Now, in finding and developing nexuses between MacEwen's and Acorn's more mythic poems with *Hogg*, I also recounted the bemused reaction of Canadian poetasters to my anthropomorphized animal poems – subjects as varied as frogs, fish, bees, butterflies, moths, snakes, bats and aggressively imperious parrots – all having been given a mythopoeic nip and tuck over the decades. I found more than a few linkages among us, as a poetic quartet, to the paranormal – meaning reincarnation, time travel, earthly apparitions and seismic sexuality, either on earth, or in prurient occurrences in hyper space. I needn't remind you of your phallocentric musings as best exemplified in "La Petite Mort," "The Gift of Tongue" and other steamy poems adroitly apportioned in your Hogg corpus.

It is clear to me that the mental and physical traumas you (through Callaghan the journalist) endured in mid-life (arrest, civil war, trial) resulted in a bardic *tour de force*, and in addition, a clutch of Hogg-driven drawings, grotesqueries that would have delighted Bellmer or Goya. Would you agree with me, in light of your own experiences, that too many of our young empire-building poetry pundits have endured little pain beyond self-induced angst, and as a result, their writings on the whole are predictable and pedestrian? They are like lovers in love with the idea of being in love, accomplished but essentially vacuous.

Hogg, my good man, I want to take up the matter of your rebirth – and ask you how and why an incarnation that should have been an inspirationally beautiful experience, as with a caterpillar transformed into a butterfly, became a monstrous experience. A kind of natal interruptus? Like a seal, you say you were hauled out of an ice hole to be savaged by ice Nazis, your soul, taken by degenerates who were working the graveyard shift:

> *Hogg came up for air.*
> *before he was half out of his hole they got him,*
> *lugged him, along the killing floor, yellow lips,*
> *jawing how he was the wrong one. bearing icons*
> *and tar the headman came and blew him a kiss.*
> *in due accordance with the law they feathered him*
> *and broke his legs. his crown was a dead pig's tit.*
> *and then, the casting of lots for his limbs.*
> *when he cried out, "Christ-quisling," they thunder-*

clapped him with a two-by-four, roped him up
by the arms between two trees and nailed
this inscription to his jawbone latch:
HERE HANGS THE KING OF THE
HATCHING DEAD.

Tell me, for all the talk of the hatching of the dead, the delivering up of the soul, can you toke up a soul? What good are souls? They certainly can't amuse us, not like dazzling exotic goldfish bubbling in an aquarium. In *Hogg*, you dream of St. Veronica after you have returned home, worn out from doing your Stations. I enjoyed reading your short pithy poem, "Hogg Dreams Veronica." I must confess to you, no stranger to confessions, that I envy your spectres. You are most fortunate to have had such illuminant company, even if she was, and still is, a dream. I feel deprived. I have yet to discern even a threadbare ghost inside or outside a dream state. I confess this as a chronic insomniac.

I have only Bombay gin martinis and my geriatric cat to keep me company in the insane hours of the morning. However, on a more serious note, what is especially puzzling to me is the partition you have set up that separates your spiritual life from your corporeally sinful secular life. In other words, as you go about the world as pilgrim and profligate, you sin prolifically – and this is to be expected, for after all, you are not a monk, but a passionate romantic bard – celebrating coitus with beautiful women. And yet, I find it mystifying that in several sections of *Hogg* you seem almost pious in your veneration of a saintly emanation of the female gender. Too impossible a virgin for my liking, too pristine, perhaps too odourless, but then in reading of your encounters with supernal females, I am rendered speechless. Ultra virgins in this age of genocidal war and environmental disasters like global warming?

I am incredulous – it seems an anachronism – this warming up to any virgin – incorporeal or corporeal. But I suppose in our multicultural society there are pockets of anachronistic virginity. Sometimes I think we would be better off going off the gold standard, substituting instead a virgin standard. I guess I am dreaming here – of impossible virgins?

I put this query to you, and it is a good starter in opening up our epistolary dialogue: Why pray on one side of the partition, only to go and compulsively sin on the other side? Is there an addictive rush associated with this bipolarity, especially after visiting a confessional? Do you not see the gross, irreconcilable contradiction in your association with the lumpen crowd as they execrate against Christ's earthly representatives – and at the same time, your acceptance of the poetry of the church – its sacred language, rites and rituals? You are not alone in erecting partitions. Milton Acorn, no matter his penchant for Stalinist agitprop, felt compelled to go against atheistic Marxism, to reinvent God, not as an androcentric sadist, a jealous God ready to incinerate revellers in Biblical cities, but as a rampaging priapic elephant deity. I have gone on too long on the matter of partitions in one's life. I should get off on the right hoof in setting a proper tone – in this, my first missive to you.

Cordially yours,
Joe Rosenblatt

HOGG AS PAINTED BY HIMSELF

A portrait does not mean a face.
There is a friendly alien hidden in our image,
our double from an invisible planet,
a visitor
who watches us as in a mournful vigil,

& when we prate loudly to ourselves
about our stale aura,
& its flickering,
this tall dunce with a conical hat
fits rainbows neatly into our retinas.

—Joe Rosenblatt

October 5

Dear Mr. Rosenblatt,

I cannot tell you how touched I am by your letter (and I know
Barry Callaghan, when he reads it, will be too), in which you
suggest that I might pull up a footstool among your frogs, fish,
bees, butterflies, moths, snakes, bats and imperious parrots – a
regular anthropomorphic pig-out.

So, to Hogg, my very own corpus.

You say that while reading my "bristly masterwork" you
found yourself sinking up to your "sloped shoulder in the ooze
of theological quicksand."

Let me say before you disappear under an overload of ooze
that Hogg only became who he was (and is) after he had folded
his shadow over his arm in Jerusalem and had learned to walk
at his own ease and at his own pace.

In other words, he had settled into his temperament, his singularity, and that singularity has its characteristics.

Unfortunately, Callaghan, who is not only a poet but also a
bit of a gadabout and rounder, has no gift for philosophical
musing. He has been known to leave the room with a bourbon
in hand if invited to join any kind of philosophical deliberation.

So be it: herein, I give you Hogg as seen by himself – a consideration of characteristics, perhaps not fully comprehended by
Barry Callaghan, that nonetheless constitute Hogg's singularity.

A predisposition to be ready for upheaval – a readiness to
be uprooted from any attachment to prejudice and/or
received opinion.

Truths, he believes, exist in correspondences. That is, in
the relationship between intellect and thing, what Thomas
Aquinas spoke of as *adaequation intellectus et rei*.

The Greek word for truth is *aletheia*, "unconcealment," and Hogg unconceals. That is, as someone constrained by his culture he nonetheless comes up, like a seal in his seal hole, with fresh and sometimes seemingly sacrilegious correspondences. He comes up with an achieved poem in which the recognizable, even the orthodox, seems not so much busted as bent. But he also certainly understands, as Heidegger said, that with every unconcealment there is an equal moment of concealment.

Our freedom is at the heart of this tension, as Heidegger goes on to say: "Freedom for what is opened up in an open region lets beings be the beings they are. Letting be always lets being be in a particular comportment which relates to them and thus discloses them, it conceals beings as a whole. Letting-be is intrinsically at the same time a concealing."

I can just hear Callaghan complaining that all this B-b-B-b-Being sounds like so much doo-wop back-up singing from the '60s! Actually, the last time I talked to Callaghan about Heidegger he started singing *Hidee-hidee-ho*, pretending he was Cab Calloway. The man lacks gravitas.

No matter. I say that what Hogg brings to this ambiguous condition of awareness is *concerned focus* (in religious terms, he is a witness).

It has been Hogg's experience that whatever he is focused on, opens up.

A simple man, Callaghan is essentially a reporter with a gift/weakness for the scatological tongue. He would say, "What I fucking-well see is who I *am*, because focused 'seeing' approaches poetry, which approaches the fucking noumenal."

However, since focused seeing is always combined with a concealment, the light of a truth is always a seed surrounded by the dark of an untruth, unconcealment by concealment.

Heidegger says this is "the mystery: not a particular mystery regarding this or that, but rather the *one* mystery."

It is this mystery that alarms the orthodox, it is this mystery that the establishment attempts to deny. It is this mystery that Hogg, always wearing the wrong shoe on the right foot, assumes is his home territory.

He is, in short, a paranoid of sorts on the road on the run (a paranoid being a man who is in possession of the facts), singing, along with the Beatles at their Heideggerian best.

Let it be!

Apparently, Hogg's hatching, his crucifixion, confounds you, but, given who Hogg is, and given his particular temperament or sensibility, a sensibility close to the gospeller John – and given who John is – "The light shines on in the dark, and the darkness has never mastered it," (John 1:5) – you might say that when we write with intense concern, we seed the dark with light.

The deeper the darkness (Josef Stalin and Stalinism), the more astonishingly luminous the moment of light (Akhmatova, Mandelstam, etc.) and Hogg, knowing this, was concerned to stay focused when he wrote about being in love in Leningrad, so that he might achieve moments (if only pin-point moments) of intensified moral apprehension, an apprehension of moral truth, just as he had tried to achieve while travelling close to the third rail through the Toronto underground system, doing his Stations of the Cross.

This is the thrust of the Jesus story as told by John, whose focus is on the play of light and dark. In this play, the little Jesus stories, the parables, do not justify or simplify the moment. The parables – as in the Woman Taken In Adultery – clarify the urgent need for awareness, a kind of informed ambiguity, an ethical awareness – and by ethical I mean a reaching out to the *other*, a reaching out, at a time, and in a place of codified values, a place of murderous normalcy. It is no accident that Pilate and Jesus are among the main characters in Bulgakov's story of Stalinist Moscow, *The Master and Margarita*: our priests, our politicians, our police are our normalcy. Jesus, as the crucified dissident, is the extreme example of the light unto the world. The urgencies he revealed, when he was on the road for the last three years of his life, were moments of Heideggerian unconcealment.

He operated, as an incredulous Hogg himself operates in Jerusalem, with an incredible openness to experience and a sense of foreordained necessity: hence, Hogg possesses an inner calm even as he is emotionally overwrought.

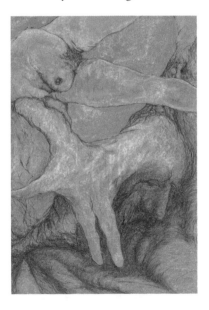

Later, when he is in Leningrad, this calm or refusal to panic, may feel, to the casual reader, like passivity, but it is not. It is apparent, upon reflection to any engaged reader, that a truth, a moment of light, does not lessen, let alone eliminate, the darkness: the darkness only changes its character and dimension. Hogg belongs to the light, is possessed by it.

Indeed, one might argue that Jesus – whoever he actually is (and if he was) – has been appropriated by his own gospellers, and, in resolving their story of his resurrection, they have given him – as Heidegger would have it – his "true" story, his freedom.

To re-state the basic proposition that is key to Hogg's predisposition: concealment and unconcealment; the lie that tells a truth, the truth that perpetuates a lie; the rational decline into aridity relieved by the orgasmic explosion of light; all this is contained in the ambiguity of the Heideggerian instance of mystery, whose dynamic lies in John's play on light and dark.

In this context, you say that you are especially puzzled by Hogg's capacity to "sin prolifically" by "celebrating coitus with beautiful women" while remaining "almost pious in his veneration of saintly…ultra virgins in this age of genocidal war…"

Well, all non-Catholics are puzzled by the Catholic capacity to lie down with, and to idealize, both the whore and the wife/mother (think of the Magdalenas and Madonnas on the walls of millions of happy homes), but Hogg is radical in his adherence to the real mystery of the Incarnation.

For him, the word made flesh is God born of woman, is God born in the blood of the womb…That's how the Incarnation narrative begins.

And the story ends, or dovetails, not just with the crucifixion of Jesus on Skull Hill, but with the three Marias at the foot of the cross, and remember that it is women to whom the angel appears, not men, to announce his Resurrection. Women at the apocalyptic moment, women at the moment of ultimate release into light. And one of those virgins was (to give the story mellow-drama) a whore!

And, one of those virgins had cuckolded her husband, taken the seed (into her vaginal ear, as is revealed in many medieval paintings). She'd "heard" the word of God. She had become the carrier of the Word made flesh. This is not a moment of saccharin empathy, angel to woman, woman to angel: this is a moment of great shock to both. And for a depiction of that shock of realizing just how far beyond the bounds of normalcy their union was, see the fantastic 14th-century sculptures by the Sienna artist, Marco Romano, in the Basilica of San Marco in Venice. Both figures express astonishment and a shudder of awe, especially the angel, at what they are about to be engaged in, the insemination of the human by the divine.

There is no separation between spirit and flesh in Hogg's sensibilia. His woman in Jerusalem gives him the gift of tongue, that is, she sucks his cock – the pentecostal and the profane at that moment mirror the metaphysical – the minaret that is in the mouth of God. Go to Rome and you will see the omnipresent obelisk habitually confronting the dome, Christ confronting his Bride the church. Or, as Thomas Aquinas would say, habit is a state of mind.

The separation of the spirit and the flesh is for puritans, Calvinists, law-givers, Jansenists, all those who treat their women as unclean, the sign of their uncleanliness being their blood: in a word, all those who have misread Paul, concentrating only on his epistle to the Romans. There are those who cannot bear the idea of the divine made flesh – hard-ons, puke, sweat, shit, drunkenness, pimples, betrayal, sickness, death. There are those who cannot bear the idea that God was at His best when He was up to His armpits in His own functionality, (the sweat, for example, upon His face caused by His carrying the cross, sweat that caused Veronica's generosity, her great gesture).

You wonder at Hogg's affinity for degenerates, albino dwarfs and spectres of all sorts. But to pursue the moment of light, as Jesus did, is to go against the grain of respectability, to go against static opinion, against orthodoxy, against the imposition of the letter of the law. In short, the status quo. The first people Jesus would drive out of the temple of today would be the representatives of Peter, the run of Popes (including John Paul II, of the Holy See, the ultimate company man, blinded and barnacled by right-wing militia men of the Americas), the Curia and the Vatican bank.

Jesus's and Hogg's companions are informers, prophets, outcasts, dissidents, Samaritans and the actual dead, like Lazarus, stinking of rot. Later, on his own cross, Hogg inverts – by wearing the unclean pig's tit as his crown – all established rituals, mirroring King Jesus, who was, after all, put to death as a slave is put to death.

The right or wrong of Jesus's death is not the issue (as right or wrong is not the issue with Hogg's crucifixion). Who killed God or who tried to crucify Hogg, is not the issue.

The issue around, and at the front of the cross, is the unconcealing of light at the moment of concealment, universal darkness. It constitutes the mystery of life in death, death in life. Knowing that Veronica, so human in her unasked-for compassion, is there, ready to wipe the face of man, of God, of the Son, as He is nailed to the light at the heart of the dark, Hogg is free in his being, free enough to let being be:

Hogg Dreams Veronica

Who is up there keeping vigil
who will wipe the face of Hogg
gaunt, unshaven, stations done,
mounts the stairs, dreams of one

who is up there keeping vigil
who will wipe the face of Hogg
cleanse his wounds, staunch the bleeding,
in her veil his pain left sleeping.

I look forward to your response.

Cordially yours,
Hogg

November 2

Mr. —— Hogg
69 Ophidian Crescent
Mimico, Ontario

Dear Mr. Hogg:

I fear that a pugilistic response to some of your views may unsettle you. In the boxing ring of intellection, it is clear that you are no roughhouse slugger; you are possessed too much by a word, "compassion"; you are of a delicate sensibilia. Though you manage to throw a few surprisingly swift philosophical jabs while waltzing effortlessly around your anticipated opponent, I suspect that your stern lyrical thrusts aren't meant to disassemble me, but only to serve as a mild didactic jarring: in other words, with your opening words to this exchange of epistles, you are trying to knock some sense into me. You are at the ready. I am at the ready. Old age hasn't mellowed my disposition: I shall try to be pugnaciously generous as I convey a "flurry of light left jabs" to your "proboscis."

Perhaps there is too much of the repressed Dionysian spirit in yours truly, being, as I am, "a wee sleekit beastie" who wants sometimes to come out of my body, to wildly dance, drink good wine, fornicate in a frenzied heat the way feral dogs conjoin, to be, if only for a moment, eternally young, as if in rebirth!

In short, perhaps I am a tad envious of your delicious sinning. If true, you must pardon the occasional, disapproving barb that I send your way. View it as seething envy on my part, envy at your runaway raptus in your quest for pleasure, envy at your having your way with a wench in some graveyard in the Holy Land. The forces of the Invisible World are indeed bewildering. You have touched the fermentive rot in my psychic

DNA. My sloped shoulders sink deeper into the quicksand of a theological muck, a muck of your making. Bear in mind that I am a grade 10 dropout, incapable of understanding the subtleties, the woof and warp of religious belief.

Nor do I want to rush, snout flaring, into political quicksand, but I take deep umbrage at your instances of bad lighting. In particular, the light you've cast upon Heidegger, so praised by Sartre and other '60s Existentialist eggheads and New Left armchair revolutionaries; Heidegger, who ratted out his Jewish colleagues and students when he was a rector for a year at the University of Freiburg in 1933. Even if you accept Heidegger's premise that in concealment there is an equal moment of unconcealment, or a revealing of *aletheia*, or truth, his equation of freedom and unconcealing truth is completely negated by his belief in the fuehrer principle!

You, on his behalf, cannot compost the camps; no sunflower doth there grow!

In accordance with the spirit of the Stoma Principium, try to imagine the cosmos as an expanding stomach in which you find Heidegger's concealing and unconcealing, his idea of truth buried in the darkness and concealed in the light, and you may well conclude that Heidegger's is a way of exploring freedom in the universe, freedom as an ongoing gluttonous eating machine: the munching, the crunching (can you not hear it?) of fast sex, alcohol, water boarding, a good toke of BC bud, rape and rapine, the mob rule of de-mobbed soldiers...veterans of venality all...even the least harmful of habits...Callaghan's compulsive putting of money on a swift nag.

Mr. Callaghan can testify to the minor mischief of the latter. You, however, are an addict of a different stripe: Hogg attached to the Heideggerian navel. I hope you're not feeding Mr. Callaghan esoteric dollops of Heideggerian antipasti. The man is too vulnerable – generous to a fault – being overly prone to imagination toxicity and expensive liquor, on a par with your unstoppable quest for whores, virgins, and paradoxically, virgins who are whores. Not to mention your bent fascination with swinish crucifixions and disquieting bouts of incantatory raving indicative of an affliction suspiciously similar to some poor sod suffering from the ravages of Tourette's syndrome. I fear, despite your reasoned tone, your honed diction, that your sanity is at the edge of some dark precipice.

Is there no way you can heave up in one great blort – in a "singular" purgative session – words like fuck, cunt, cock-sucking (your "gift of tongue") and other slurs against decorum, and get it all out of your system? Such words no longer carry the charge of dark mysteries, the mysteries of the unsayable, the rapture caused in the hamstrings that can leave lovers shaking: no, they are now just common words uncommonly crude. As you might say, "For fuck's sake, give it fucking well up or fuck off."

In this temper of mind, I am deeply suspicious of your "angelic linkages." But I suppose there is no conflict or partition betwixt a fine Barry Callaghan-fuelled potation and an ethereal

Virgin? Even monks drink, perhaps not to the extent of our mutual friend, Mr. Callaghan; and yet how many of the hoody brethren can claim, as you do, to have witnessed an angelic illumination in the wee hours of the morning, exhausted after doing your Stations?

Singularity, Hogg, I suspect is your favourite word. As a force within your porcine potential, it seems to open up pathways of truth – truth being your Aquinas-inspired *adaequation intellectus et rei* – pathways down which you, the "uprooter," unearth the unconcealed truth, your "aletheia." Small wonder I have a fear of Latin. I find it chilling that you, oh blasphemer of the cloven hoof, as you pursue truth in all its sacredness, delve so easily into the sacrilegious. As if the sacrilegious was not only natural to you, but was inherent in truth itself.

Yes, there is no doubt: the unborn poem is deeply concealed. Yes, suddenly, in the mercurial rush of a moment, the poem is unconcealed – revealed, born on the page (as opposed to composed) and with that spent orgasmic moment, the tension dissipates, just as it does, I reckon, in complete coitus? There is also much to be said on behalf of your Hogg-styled catechism – wherein you maintain your "ambiguous condition of awareness in *concerned focus*" – in religious terms, of course. Let's leave Mr. Callaghan out of the Heidegger mystery. Let me assure you that Mr. Callaghan is no simple man. I might add he may well share my dark suspicion of a Heideggerian pony who goes by the name of "one mystery." The latter I find strangely poetic, like the Trinity, which for a corrupted secular being like myself is entirely unsettling, totally puzzling.

Like a horse wearing "the wrong shoe," Mr. Hogg, you are in the wrong: the paranoid man is not in possession of the facts. If the light of unconcealment is concealed from him, and then, suddenly, the facts come shining in, he will still imagine that *they* are after him, and who's to say *they* aren't? *They* is the variable. Your paranoid man is certainly "on the road on the run," but the question is, from whom? You have your paranoid man "singing along with the Beatles at their Heideggerian best, Let it be." Would this paranoid man – could it be you, Mr. Hogg – presently be wearing an aluminum beanie to ward off death rays?

And now to another weightier matter, one that leaves me, as a secular pagan, somewhat discomforted. You are right in stating that I am confounded by Hogg's "hatching, his crucifixion, as a beginning..."

What to make of your "gospeller John," who said that, "The light shines on in the dark, and the darkness has never mastered it," (John 1:5). I, myself, have written out of "intense concern," but I am still waiting in the deep darkness for a bioluminescent flock of ultra-virgins to appear. I plead secular ignorance on the matter of darkness, having never mastered the light. Nonetheless, I think I understand the precept, and if it means that truth is the light that darkness – meaning we humans – fail to grasp, then I begrudgingly find myself in agreement with your idea of unconcealment, but only if you agree that "prolific sinning, celebrating coitus with beautiful women" (my words) – is out of alignment with the familial tranquility of "Magdalenas and Madonnas on the walls of millions of happy homes" (your words). Yes, I am puzzled! You say that "Hogg is radical in his adherence to the real mystery of the Incarnation." Whores and virgins, I can understand, but not in a worshipful way. I suspect you harbour a fantasy, that you are made in the image of the Christ crucified on Skull Hill, sharing the intimate camaraderie of the two thieves.

But doesn't modesty – or some semblance of it – prevent you from wanting to be worshipped by the three Marias? The divine word made flesh I can understand poetically, but why must you incorporate the corporality of the fleshy word? Why must you imbue it with "hard-ons, puke, sweat, shit, drunkenness, betrayal, sickness, death," and other bodily indiscretions? Taking your logic to its final conclusions, do you, in the act of coitus and during the "gift of tongue," think of excretions? Is this how you experience the little death of the orgasm? You are correct in assuming I and other puritans believe in the separation of spirit and flesh. But you go a step too far in assuming that "God was at His best – when He was most human – was up to His armpits in His own bodily functions." You must have a direct line to the Creator himself in your presumptions.

-PARTY TIME-

I question the company you keep, your "affinity for degenerates, albino dwarfs, and spectres of all sorts…" I am revolted by any idealization of the lumpen crowd. What to make of your Medusa among the Moochers, your delusional Sisyphus – all those social cankers who have destroyed entire working-class neighbourhoods by leaving their excrement and dirty needles in laneways and in sandboxes of children's playgrounds? I wish I could teleport you to Vancouver's downtown east side, starting with Main and Hastings – and let you revel in your plague of Medusas and Moochers who would sell their mother for a hit of crack cocaine. Just the sight of them is enough to give me hives.

-DEMON LOVE-

Though I laud your stern sense of justice when you suggest that "the first person Jesus would drive out of the temple of today would be the representatives of Peter, the Popes," I wonder if you would also block a hooker from plying her trade at the Temple's golden door? Am I to imagine you as the sacred bouncer and moral guardian of the Temple? You take on far too many duties. Nonetheless, I believe that your Heideggerian notion of light and darkness, concealment and unconcealment is appropriate to the telling of "the truth" about the nature of Stalinist tyranny. I agree that "the deeper the darkness (Josef Stalin and Stalinism), the more astonishingly luminous was the moment of light (Akhmatova, Mandelstam, etc.). This was and is frighteningly true in totalitarian states. Your experiences in Leningrad bear you out, bear out the potency of your "little

Jesus stories." Parables lend themselves to a "kind of informed ambiguity" – "an ethical awareness." How else can one operate in a society where the secret police, having been educated in "codified values," are able to interpret the inner meanings of parables, to decode the double meanings in poems? This is how the poet Osip Mandelstam found out that Stalin couldn't take a joke. Convicted of counter-revolutionary activities, Osip perished in the Gulag Archipelago in the '30s. This is what comes of having an educated Stalinist satrapy operating in a mode of Heideggerian unconcealment so that they are able to liquidate enemies of the state.

I hope you are not too discomfited by my jibes meant to test your mettle. View my transgressions as yet another instance of unambiguous moments of vigorous unconcealment. Let it be!

Cordially yours,
Joe Rosenblatt

December 9

Dear Joe:

While reading your letter I was reminded of lines from a recent poem by John Ashbery,

> *The herringbone is floating eagerly up*
> *From the herring to become a parquet.*

(Callaghan, of course, has little time for Ashbery.) After a brisk waltz on your parquet, I managed to get back to the bone of our contention.

Which is: your determined assertion that Hogg is not who I say he is, but who you say he is, a "divided Hogg."

You have been insistent.

So, let me come at the matter freshly. With a little radical common sense: *il senso commune della nostra medisima mente umana.*

Callaghan likes to quote Matthew Arnold: "The job of the poet is to try to see the thing for what it is in and of itself." And I like to say, "God is in those things, God is in the details."

Hogg is my name, detail is my game.

As a detail man, Hogg, like Bobby Dylan, has forgotten more details than he remembers. In "My Life in a Stolen Moment," Dylan says:

> *I can't tell you the influences 'cause there's*
> *too many to mention an' I might*
> *leave one out.*
>
> *An' that wouldn't be fair*
> *Woody Guthrie, sure*

Big Joe Williams, yeah
It's easy to remember those names
But what about the faces you can't find again
What about the curbs an' corners an' cut-offs
That drop out of sight and fall behind
What about the records you hear but one time
What about the coyote's call and the bulldog's bark
What about the tomcat's meow an' milk cow's moo
An' the train whistle's moan
Open up yer eyes an' ears an' yer influenced
An' there's nothing you can do about it

Hogg, eyes and ears open, is never ideologically confrontational. *A priori* ain't his game.

He remains calm, incredulous, as he absorbs the incredible. He exists (in the Sartrean sense) because he has become (in the Lacanian sense) his own narrative.

And so, within my narrative, there are no polarities. When Hogg first set out for the land of the desert sun, singing that old dark blues song *The night time is the right time*, he said he was seeking his own singularity. That singularity turned out to be mysterious, mysterious yet simple – as, for example, the Trinity is mysterious yet simple. The medieval holy man, Adam of St. Victor, said the mystery of the Trinity is contained in a walnut.

Hogg stands upright as if he were confessing to himself in a mirror. He knows that behind him there are shadows, and on the other side of the mirror, there are shadows in the dark.

He is the Father talking to the Son, while in the shadows – seeded by light, the Holy Spirit – there are presences who whisper in his ear: words, stories, prophecies, the shadow presences of the Real Presence, the Son, who is not the alter ego of the Father but is One with the Father. The shadows are his angels, as the French poet Max Jacob wrote:

It may be a strange dream
seized you tonight.
You thought you saw an angel
And it was your mirror.

Hogg's angels are his saints: Urreal, Medusa, Lazarus, Rasputin, John the Conqueroo, Akhmatova...

Or, without becoming too theologically playful...

Hogg has a Hegelian streak: thesis talking to antithesis, with the shadow of a synthesis (an old story) behind him and the shadow of a new synthesis (a new story) ahead of him. So that his narrative as he knows it, and exists in it, is a continuous walking through his own mirror to get – like the proverbial chicken – to the mystery of the other side. However, he goes from Purgatory through Hell to Purgatory. Hogg has the metaphorical *modus vivendi* of John the gospeller but he has no substantial interest in a final destination or resolution. And neither is he interested in the Apocalypse or Paradise. He doesn't need an apocalypse. He doesn't need Heaven. He needs a drink.

So, any way you hack it, Hogg is at one with himself, and the key to his personality (his several persons) is his readiness to redefine everyone in relation to changing possibilities.

As he moves about in his state of readiness, keep this in mind: Hogg's paranoia is entirely reasonable. He knows that he stands in the *shining*, in the light, one aspect of his temperament at a time while the rest of his porky self is in darkness. In the dark is the Shadow, and as Lamont Cranston explained to his radio audience in the '40s, to all of us little children, there are truths "only the Shadow knows" about the things that go bump in the dark night of the soul.

Related to this is his complete acceptance of the possible: what happens when you "open up yer eyes an' ears an' yer influenced." That is, he is entirely open to the Law of Unintended

Consequences: out of abominations and abhorrent acts great delicacy and beauty can come, or as my friend and street prophet Judas Priest has it, if you ask "why the kiss is the ancient invitation to the abyss," the answer is, "by betrayal the beautiful is begun." Judas wears the face of Jesus, no matter his disgrace.

When the mirror-wise Hogg sees himself, he sees a sybaritic poet who is also the red-headed stranger, Iscariot[1], who has just "blowed in your town" (Iscariot meaning red-haired stranger from Cyprus). Hogg, on the run, confronts at every turn a partial revelation, a new mysterium.

Which brings me to your hackle-raising over Heidegger.

I am astonished.

You, least of all, should confuse a man's everyday blundering in politics with his visioning powers (*pace* Ezra Pound, adrift in his Sargasso Sea of contradictions). Think of yourself, the gentlest of men, wearing a black band on your soul in memory of your dead pussycat. You are perhaps the least, physically violent man I know and yet you are the nation's self-declared poet of Sturm and Stoma,[2] chief advocate for ingurgitation, chief advo-

---

[1] Listen to Willie Nelson's lament for the red-headed stranger in his song sequence, "Tougher Than Leather."

[2] Ingurgitation, Stoma, as a biological imperative lying at the heart of human aggression, has pedigree. Edmund Wilson (a model of intellectual integrity for Callaghan), suggested in the preface to his great study of the American Civil War – *Patriotic Gore* – that the military industrial north could not help but ingurgitate the agrarian south in the same manner as he had seen a giant sea slug devour a smaller sea slug in a 1950s Walt Disney film, and he further upset the liberal optimists of his time by arguing that "moral issues" – like slavery – were, and always have been, attachments to this "swallowing" – attachments that provided cause and allowed for justification. This filling of the stomach, Stoma, should not, however, be confused with the treatise by Archimedes called the Stomachion, (pronounced sto-MUCK-yon). Only recently recovered, the Stomachion deals with combinatorics (and it is through recent advances in computer science that we've been able to understand what Archimedes was up to), an approach to "possibilities" that is entirely in tune with Hogg's temperament. Simply

cate for Stoma, the stomach, as the inexorable, devouring first
principle of life.[3]

It is true and regrettable, even appalling, that so finely tuned
a sensibility as Heidegger should have hung his hat on Hitler's
head and then kept a silence about it till he died. [4]

---

put, Archimedes was trying to see how many ways 14 irregular strips of
paper could be put together to make a square (the answer – 17, 152 –
requires a careful, systematic counting of all possibilities). Hogg might ask,
why 14 and why a square? As he might ask, why 12 apostles and why three
crucified with the three Marias at the foot of the Cross? He might. But not
likely: what he's interested in are possibilities, taking the given situation –
14 strips of paper – as he encounters it.

[3] I have made a most unlikely discovery in a work by Callaghan's old friend,
the love poet of Jerusalem, Yehuda Amichai. It is in *Travels of Benjamin of
Tudela*, a hymnal moment testifying to the sound of swallowing, testifying
to history as bowel sounds in the intestinal tract:

The sound of swallowing is the sound of history
belch and hiccup and crunching of bones
these are the sounds of history,
bowel movements – its movement. Digestion.
In digesting, all begin to be alike:
brother and sister, man and dog, saint and sinner,
flower and cloud, shepherd and sheep, all governor
and governed, all descend into sameness.
My experimental life descends too.
All descends into the terrible sameness. All is fruit
of the intestinal tract.

[4] I think you might at least try to be as open to Heidegger as Paul Celan was.
His poem, "Todtnauberg," takes its title from the place where Heidegger lived:

Arnika, eyebright, the
draft from the well with the
starred die above it…

After the war, Celan kept up a thoughtful relationship with the
philosopher despite Heidegger's refusal to break his silence, to take back his
praise of the Nazi regime. Celan's poem is a reaching out, a yearning – as
was the inscription of his name that he left in Heidegger's "visitors" book –
it was his ongoing hope for a word of atonement:

the line inscribed
in that book about
a hope, today,
of a thinking man's
coming word
in the heart…

But I was trying to make a point, not about Heidegger and his cotton-candy prose, but about the mysterium, the universe that is eternal even as it is created. As Hogg sees it, the mysterium is in everything that he encounters – an unveiling that leads not to judgement, not to the laying down of civil, criminal and moral laws, but to a dawn that seeds even death with hope.

Death,
like the night,
only darkens
the
door
of
day
at dawn
long
enough
to
disappear

As Hogg enters each day, he knows that meaning is what we endeavour to bring to life. There is no meaning independent of our trying to make fresh sense out of everything we encounter – to colour things in a human light (Callaghan's friend, the French poet and *aficionado* of bull fighting, Robert Marteau, has suggested that God is a *White Light* and by moving through stained glass that white light becomes stained light – God is then able to reveal Himself to be atone with the human condition).

Or, as Hogg put it in Leningrad:

It all begins at the end.
We know what love is
When it's over,

The trail of two people
Bending into the echo of their own laughter
across a lake fresh with snow.
"And this, this," she cried, looking back,
"is the whiteness of God's mind.
Without us he is nothing.
Nichevo, nichevo. *"*

This staining, this human light, can be the light of Botticelli but it can also be horrific.

Hogg is no fool. He knows Mr. Kurtz is not dead. Hogg knows there are ruthless fathers who fish for their own sons, as hunters fish for seals:

Hogg saw
ice inlaid in light
along the canal

and old men
fishing
for their sons

under birch trees
hung
with the severed tongues

of bells tolled
at
Lubyanka

where bodies were laid out
pearled with blood
beside

skinning bowls
made from the silver spoons
of those

who died
looking for air
holes

in the ice
filled with blue
sky and hooks.

Hogg knows that the blue sky of compassion *sans* hooks is rare.

He knows this for a good reason. He has been out into the enemy camp. He has tried to look straight into the eyes of other men, the shadow-makers – from the absolute evil-doers, Pol Pot, Stalin, Hitler, to high-end killers like Milosoviç, all the way down to your garden-variety thugs like Bull Connor with his cattle prod, Ariel Sharon with his swagger stick or Ian Paisley of the Red Hand. He has tried to look straight into their self-justifying, blather stories about themselves.

Because he knows that a story full of lies tells a true story about the liar.

He knows that justified sinners are often the least justified, and he knows that the least rewarded passion is compassion.

When Hogg keeps watch beside those fishing holes in the ice, he knows the meaning of "Himmler's Law," that God, in a merciless act, planned and committed the first genocide. He killed not just the "perps," but all of the citizens of Sodom, unto the very last Sodomite in his or her mother's womb, and for what? For the crime of *being*. And that is what is so appalling about the killing of the Jews: they were killed not for what they did, but for *being*. Then the Lord God of Stoma rewarded his man Lot – who had first offered his virgin daughters up for a good fucking and then fucked them himself – with tribal lands while, out in the hills, Abraham, picking sand lice out of his hair, watched in a spell of Heideggerian silence.

Hogg knows that such stories are the signifying moral stories of his culture, and he lives with that knowledge, and in that knowledge, he tries to see those stories for what they are.

His insight into genocide is a shining moment for Hogg, a seeing of the story for what it is. And that's all he wants: to be able, in a pig-sized *Lebensraum,* to say what his common sense tells him. In awe of all right-minded skinners and flayers, Hogg rose up, and set out in search of a sacred place, Jerusalem, where he'd heard the last word on the dice might be Holy Holy Holy.

He learned, however, that the God he sought lives not in the Holy Land but at home, in himself. That was his unveiling unto himself, the moment – in a silence beyond words – when he was reborn. He was possessed by the mysterium, for which he found corresponding images in his drawings. And here is a point about Hogg – this is where he steps away from Heidegger: he is not submissive to the mystery of Being. Neither is he politically submissive to a state or tribe or any *Ubermensch.* No, Hogg becomes less moral as he becomes more ethical, more assertive as he becomes more tolerant, more intellectually engaged as he becomes more detached, more idiosyncratic and idealistic as he settles into an acceptance of a society of cynics and sapheads.

Having found himself by doing his Stations of the Cross from Sheppard Station to Union Station, Hogg – at "home" – feels free enough audacious enough, vulgar enough, sardonic enough, to cry, "Behold the Whole Hogg."

Yours fondly,
Hogg

January 8

Mr. ——— Hogg
69 Ophidian Crescent
Mimico, Ontario

Dear Mr. Hogg,

Your letter to me of December 9th seems darker than usual. I
begin this epistle by assuring you that you're not alone in your
paranoia. My own paranoia, like yours, is "entirely reasonable."
In speaking of those "shadowy presences" – presences you per-
ceive to be "seeded by the light of the Holy Spirit" – why do you
appropriate the umbrageous Lamont Cranston, the fabled radio
phantom of the '40s (known simply as the Shadow to a rapt and
terrified audience of children), to your own private stock of
head-haunting shadows? I don't mind you quoting the New
York bard, John Ashbery, marine witness to the parquetry of
herring on the ocean surface,

The herringbone is floating eagerly up
From the herring to become a parquet...

But why? I take your use of Ashbery as a witty red herring. So
let's move on to your bone of contention.

It is true I deemed you a divided Hogg. A more apt descrip-
tion would be: "a creature who is one part pure lamb and one
part predacious cougar." Your "irreconcilable polarities," passive
aggressive duality – possibly what shrinks define as bipolar disorder – is not part pure lamb and part predacious cougar, not if
I am to read your partition correctly. I don't consider a sex addict
to be a voracious flesh-eating predator. I think your personality
embodiment is, by far, more on the mutton side.

You are a self-confessed sex addict, bordering on the infantile, especially when let loose among your sacred virgins, especially the one seen taking the medieval holy seed into her ear. That she is in the act of committing adultery passes through me like a magic bullet – but this doesn't make you an intractable, famished cougar stalking young prey. I think you are more in the line of a fluffy domestic feline, not a feral big cat in oestrus. Do be gentle with your analogous self.

I am open to examining your Hoggish-Heideggerian axioms of light and darkness and I am eager that the truth, in its many guises, be unconcealed. I think, however, we should leave Mr. Callaghan and his obsession with quoting Matthew Arnold to his own devices and humour the man as to whether "God is in the details." Why assume God is in the details? He might be on His knees in some time worm tunnel digging Himself into the Stoma of a parallel universe – and consequently, He would have no time for mere details. Would you pester the numinous Master of parquets with silly details? You are unquestionably the "detail Hogg" with your penchant for quoting obscure celebrity mind-speculators – Jesus with his scrumptious parables, Mr. Callaghan (estimable tippler with a passion for the ponies), Bobby Dylan, or many among our marginalized societal scum. I hear a fiendish laugh down the corridors of my waning septuagenarian brain. It's Lamont Cranston of blessed memory.

You have been too unintentionally comedic, especially in your angelic associations, your correspondences: "Medusa, Lazarus, Rasputin, John the Conqueroo, Akhmatova…" What an odd admixture: a snaky-haired goddess who could turn your friendly neighbourhood coiffure into stone, a holy leper that Christ laid his healing hands upon, a Russian faith-healing priest who was a spiritual advisor to the Czar and Czarina, a marginalized Toronto street Bedouin, and a victim of Stalin's dystopia; all your sainted angels, joined together in some puzzling assemblages. What am I to conjecture here? You didn't toke up, by chance, before starting your letter?

However, luminosity aside, you do sometimes speak the "porky" truth, Mr. Hogg. Paranoia is grounded firmly in the concrete of reality. You are right on the flaring snout when you state: "Just because you are paranoid doesn't mean they are not trying to get you." True, so damned bristly true! Yet, do I detect a scintilla of disapproval from you in my "hackle-raising over Heidegger," a certain passive irritability? It isn't just Heidegger that raises my hackles, it is (to repeat myself) your amalgam of "saints" that sends me into a spinning gyre. You have Medusa down as an angel alongside the mad monk Rasputin, who is linked to the poet Akhmatova through John the Conqueroo and Doctor Ded. You have become far too tied to the fascia of contradiction, too attached to an absurd irreconcilable disunity, in the Hegelian sense.

You state: "Hogg, eyes and ears open is influenced but never ideological," and then you turn around and paradoxically state: "He remains calm, incredulous, as he absorbs the incredible. He exists (in a Sartrean sense) because he has become (in the Lacanian sense) his own narrative." I won't labour the Lacanian, since the unconscious is another language all its own, but to state in the next breath that within your narrative "there are no polarities," is a conflictive appositional nexus: you are theological, and yet have more mud on your hooves than any of Mr. Callaghan's winning nags.

What has Sartre got to do with it, and how does he fit into your narrative that contains no narratives? You are a licentiously secular contradiction wrapped in an enchilada of Christology, and I can't see the twain meeting up like a viper biting its own tail in a zero of contradiction. Also, I do wish you would stop involving Mr. Callaghan in your rather baffling, off-track mystagogy. I am

trying to wean him off drink and I fear you can only drive him
to drink – with your talk of "singularity," especially when it
comes to that medieval holy man, your beloved Adam of St.
Victor, who apparently claimed that the mystery of the Trinity
is contained in a walnut. Some walnut!

You have pressed all the right buttons in me, Mr. Hogg. My
tusky truth turns head-on to meet the split hooves of your logic
as you portion out parity in evildoing.

Your bizarre historical connections really grab my snout of
contention. You have that alpha Hebrew patriarch, Abraham,
picking sand lice from his hair, while observing Lot in "Heideggerian silence" offering up "his virgin daughters for a good fucking."

A quick aside: being no authority on the Bible, I will pass
on Lot's questionable incest. Am I, however, to call for a fatwa
against you for impugning Abraham's beard? I caution you,
muffle your views, particularly while travelling through an
Islamic country, where they take Abraham and his beard seri-
ously. Also, I ask you to be respectfully mindful that the
Abrahamic line (lice and all) leads to your own Awesome Crew,
to the "Real Presence, the Son, who is not the alter ego of the
Father, but is One with the Father."

I believe that the sudden fate of the fun-loving twisted citizens of Sodom had more to do with a natural seismic occur-
rence, a rogue fault line going awry deep in the earth's crust,
than the Lord's fiery Final Solution to the Sodomite Question,
what you so succinctly term, "Himmler's Law."

Human mayhem, past and present, is as natural to humankind as a camel tonguing a salt lick, a gift of tongue, so to speak.
I mean no disrespect to Lot's wife, but wasn't she warned by God
that if she turned and witnessed the destruction of Sodom and
Gomorrah, she would be turned into a pillar of salt "for camel's

to lick?" We can't always protect people from their own folly (as I cannot protect you from the folly of associating Sharon with Milosoviç). God's punitive style is merely the mirror image of man's inhumanity to man. Evil is in the genome, ready to combust in all its fury under the right conditions. Going by the First Stomaic Law of Historical Ingurgitation, I ask you: who in fifty years will remember the eight hundred thousand Tutsis exterminated by the Hutus in a brief hundred-day period in 1994, while the UN, that "Family of Nations," did nothing to stop the genocide?

I think we can agree that throughout the millennia, individuals who have revolutionized the way we view philosophy, physics, metaphysics, poetry and the like, invariably harbour an unpleasant opaque side, until it becomes unconcealed. And there is something to be said for your poetic reaffirmation regarding the whiteness of God's mind. I sense a play of intense spiritual light that acts as a balancing counterpoint – particularly in its application to your depictions of the victims of the Stalinist terror – to that darkly nightmarish victimology you have so impeccably detailed in your last published *Hogg, the Seven Last Words*. Perhaps only the Shadow does know what evil lurks in the hearts of men.

What perplexes me throughout the whole of the Hogg epic is your strident humanity. It irks me – not the gusty political linkages, and your political naiveté in general – but the bubbliness of it all! It is an irritant, small in the scale of effervescent dialectics, but nevertheless, an irritant. However, I am learning to adapt; I realize that it is part and parcel of who you are in your partitioned being. Your Leningrad experience has unhinged the "human light" in you. You are a traveller into your own heart of darkness: I grant you that the Mr. Kurtz in Hogg is not dead, as sure as "there are ruthless fathers who fish for their own sons, as hunters fish for seals." True, how sadly true, and monstrous mothers who eat their own sons.

And sadly true are your intuitive reminiscences of Stalinist Russia, the horrors that took place inside Lubyanka prison, a neo-baroque building with parquet floors and light piss-green walls, a horrifically infamous institution for torturing prisoners deemed "enemies of the people." Imagine the blood of victims running over those beautiful parquet floors! You have heard their screams. Admittedly, your Russian experience was an enrichment, an agglutination of concealment and unconcealment: a babushka doll unconcealing stacked diminutive dolls within dolls.

As we proceed in our vigorously challenging epistles to convey a cross-fertilization of enriched intellectual pollen, each to each, I find myself becoming a little unglued. Perhaps we are both becoming unglued. A voice within assures me that there is nothing to be alarmed about. I wander through life with a gimp left foot and an increasing neuropathy that no MRI can locate.

If I aim to separate the carnally starved, sinful boy from his purer essence, meaning the ultra-virginally clean soul, then you are right in calling me a puritan – because of my belief that the soul and body are in conflict. And yours aren't, I suppose? You believe in the absolute singularity of body and soul – their insep-arability. There isn't much more I can say to convince you that the soul far outweighs the value of the body shell – in spiritual currency, that whether you are given the Gift of Tongue, or a gift of natural coitus, I declare, and shall keep doing so, that the body is corruptible, but the soul is there forever, like death and taxes.

Whether one views the cosmos as a fixed, though mutable-sparkly ocean, or as a multiple universe in flux, isn't it logical to think that the chances of souls conjoining will increase in any meeting up with our cosmic twin along the Milky Way? Working the actuary/probability table out in multiple progres-sion, even at the low end – the power of ten – it stands to rea-son that with the more universes we encounter, the more our souls will go begging for a polarity date. Millions of years will pass, and that cosmic dance card will be always full of fluttering heartthrobs wanting to spiral or whirl around some ballroom in deep space as conjoining twins. No gift of tongue in hyperspace! Pardon my views on spirit transport. I am clearly obsessed by this question as you are obsessed with the Holy Spirit. Let us admit it: we want to be continually reborn, because we are plainly scared of the finality of death. I won't raise the issue of reincarnation, for that would be toking up on some substance stronger than reality.

You, and Gwendolyn MacEwen and I – and to a very minor extent, Milton Acorn (via his supernal pachyderm stoned on stellar testosterone) – have raised the meaning of soul transport to a vertiginous new height, with one possible exception, your "alchemic" influence, the French poet, Robert Marteau (whom Mr. Callaghan brilliantly translated into English), and his fine notion that God is white light. I am intrigued by this fierce white light. Does it sizzle around the Throne of God? Have you seen this light? What does it all mean?

Be forewarned: God, being both a merciful and a vengeful Creator, might be carrying a grudge: recall your bit in Hogg – where you observe (on consecrated ground of all places, from a church grave in the Holy Land) a minaret towering into God's mouth? I think God would draw an electro-magnetic line on this abuse of poetic licence; you have gone over that line in questioning His omnipresent, righteous heterosexuality. The Lord, unlike those poetasters we find in the small pond of Canadian poetry, is a meticulous indwelling reader: fleshed out words mean something to Him. As a precaution, before going into that Long Night, I would advise you to wear an asbestos suit. By the way, when was the last time you stepped into a confessional box, that is, if, metaphorically speaking, you are in earnest in utilizing some of those stations of Toronto's subway system as your Stations of the Cross? Perhaps you might consider "Stations" in the tunnelled subway line in deep space. Imagine a rapid transit system infinitely faster than the speed of our average star racing across the Milky Way. Who knows if wormholes actually exist? They could be time tunnels. But conceivably, you my friend, could do those Stations for all Eternity. I am sure that some of your more acidulous critics would advocate your being served with a fatwa for calling into question God's sexual orientation.

To move on: you say that the nighttime is the right time for you. This makes perfect sense to me, because the night is so conducive to Spirit time. And who knows, other than Lamont Cranston, what evil lurks behind some stairwell, or in a bedroom where a tired earthling, such as you, might chance upon an unexpected illumination? You have at least done something creative with your early morning hours. But in my case, the nighttimes brings the curse of insomnia. I do derive some benefits from my affliction: deer bathed by lunar light come into view outside my window, or I am transfixed by an owl swooping suddenly down from a half-lit highway lamppost to prey upon a passing vole, and for a moment I entertain the possibility that this splendid nocturnal bird, with its humungous wingspan, could be a winged apparition; or I envision a pulsating light I see moving across the starry sky as some alien craft, a flying cat, for what else could it be at that ungodly hour?

As for the appearance of night light illumination on the page, I prefer your poem, "La Petite Mort," and its sublime language…

I lay down in the sky
with the moon in my throat, sleeping,
and undid my nightmares
only to find
a chalk light had come

into your eyes,
the light a man sees
when a woman dies a little
with the pain
of
a
pleasure
he cannot sustain
in her.

As memory serves me, the coarseness of "The Gift of Tongue" leaves little to the imagination of any thinking romantic protoplasm. Such night illumination has also been shed upon your poem, "What Does Darkness Know?" – a poem worthy of any prestigious anthology of contemporary English poetry, a shining upon you, fallen in love with the seed-pearl light in a desert woman's dream. May I purchase that line?

When you quote John:1:5, "the light shines on the dark, and the darkness has never mastered it," I believe you really have mastered the darkness, while staring down the hideous black dog.

Your poem not only affirms the light, but also celebrates joyous luminosity, and it is a light that is your protector, for it continually negates the darkness.

At this juncture of our discourse, however, I feel an obligation to warn you about toxic levels of imagining. Your kinetic language, rich in subliminal nutrients, leaves you at risk of falling victim to chromatic raptus, and mental defoliation. I am sure you are aware that the Immortal Bards were often afflicted with image poisoning. And in *their* exploratory quest for the whole hog (no offence intended) they were manically driven to the borders of the laughing crickets. Some of the greatest English-language poets (with help from dollops of opium or the "green fairy" of absinthe) have suffered psychotic episodes in their ingestion of cathartic images flavoured with erogenous condiments.

Their excessive binging on bioluminescent imaginings is not unlike the after-effects of lead poisoning experienced by the early master painters, or lowly house painters. Your long poem is hallucinatory in places, so I do suspect you suffer from toxic imaging. I am reminded of the early 19th-century rusticated poet John Clare. This "peasant" bard, as the snot-nosed bourgeois poets and intellectuals of the period typified him, suffered a psychotic breakdown. But it was more than mere imagination contaminating his rapture about songbirds in the thickets. A widower, having to support seven children, he suffered a complete nervous collapse and was incarcerated in a lunatic asylum, declared by his doctor, who went by the unlikely name of Skrimshaw, to be "naturally insane after years addicted to poetic prosing."

An early 18th-century judge at the London Old Bailey, Lord Bacon, trying a condemned prisoner by the name of Hogg, took umbrage at that poor wretch's plea for mercy. Hogg had urged him to commute his sentence of death to life in prison. He had played the porcine card. After all, wasn't he a Hogg and His Worship, Lord Bacon? They had much in common, he pleaded. Alas, the remark tweaked a funny nerve ending in the stoma of that judicious servant of the law, who replied that a good shank of hog had to be "hung and stretched to be good bacon."

The Stoma of civilization at times demands a taut rope, or face the acid reflux that comes with civil disorder. By the beard of Abraham, you have got my goat. So let the bristles of unconcealment merrily fly! Forgive my barbed, verbose hooks that have lodged in your piggish flesh. This is my way, in a moment of singularity.

Cordially yours,
Joe Rosenblatt

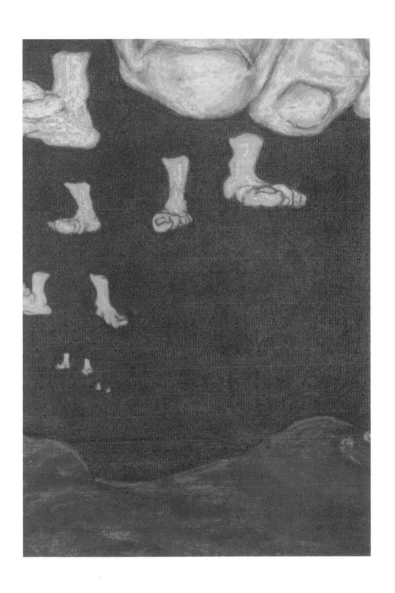

April 15

Dear Mr. Rosenblatt:

I must say, your response to my epistles has been delightful, dense, comforting in its pugnacity – a flurry of light left jabs *bip bip bip bip* – to my proboscis.

I have been, perhaps, too "philosophical" in my recent ruminations (Callaghan thought so; he has told me in no uncertain terms that I am a priggish little prick), but be that as it may, once more into the breach I go – on tiptoe – through my own tulips.

So, about the *mysterium* and my interest in the idea of *unconcealing.*

You have been provoked. Let me be clear. I know that the mysterium is an abstraction, and that, as an abstraction, it can become a giant devouring slug. And I know that such ingurgitation tempts fascism.

I know this.

And I know that Heidegger with all his talk about Being – the talk that talks to itself of itself – tied himself openly and determinedly to the tyranny of despotic nationalism, to the idea of blood destiny, to Hitler and the Nazi Party.

I know this, but Heidegger, *he dead and gone, Mr. Bones.*

I choose to pick through his brainpan.

To my advantage.

As I do, for example, with Ezra Pound, your favourite slime ball: my revenge on Pound is not exacted by ignoring him; nor do I cast him out like a devil. I take what I can learn from his great gifts – his lucid line, his musical dexterity – and turn those gifts against the fascist ideas he espoused; against all levels of State and Party thuggery in our time.

Like Adorno, I am as fascinated by Heidegger, as I am repelled by him.

Like Hannah Arendt, I have come to entertain the possibility of forgiveness (no matter his steadfast silence after the war) but also I insist on his culpability. Is that the scintilla of disapproval you need?

But forgiveness?

Yes!

The approach toward forgiveness is a matter of temperament. Fundamentally, I believe forgiveness is something that you do first *for yourself* – you bite clean through your own umbilical cord, a cord that is attached to your own disgust or need to justify yourself. It is a bloodline attachment that gives your enemy not just a hold on you, but the power to punish you by compelling you, through guilt, to punish yourself.

With respect to punishment (justice) and forgiveness, you might look at a slight but charming Callaghan story in *The Black Queen* collection, "Spring Water."

It is a simple story: an old priest is ambling around town, talking as he walks. He stops in front of the federal police headquarters, a huge concrete bunker, and says, "To tell you the truth, it's always been a weakness of mine, the police. I can understand how a man can become a thief or a car salesman or just out-and-out shiftless, or even a priest, but I cannot understand why a man would want to be a policeman. A priest, after all, if he's any good at what he's doing and if he's not a dope, is engaged in forgiveness. But a policeman, if he's any good, is always putting the arm on a man. Punishment, plain and simple…there has to be punishment and people who do the punishing, but I just can't understand a man wanting to do that with his life. It's the wanting to punish that puzzles me."

Which brings me around to bullies, thugs, and pugs. You sprang a small leak over the "folly" of my mention of Sharon.

Let me say this (since, I alone, poor fool that I am, chose to put my cloven hoof down in Jerusalem):

As I see Zionism, there was from the beginning a will among Zionists to do something redemptive, to redeem the land by returning to it as a homeland.

There was also a will to do something destructive – a will from the beginning to redeem the land by returning to clear the land of its indigenous people. (Hogg recalls the unambiguous words of Jabotinsky and Begin and their general, Ygal Allon, of the Palmach in the Galilee...and Golda Meir, who looked Callaghan in the eye in 1970 in a CBC interview and told him that the Palestinians would be "forgotten in twenty years.")

Callaghan's straightforward point since 1969 has been this: since the Palestinians are increasingly there, you either deal with them or you'll have to pen them up or kill them. And if they are there, they will resist. You can call them Ray and you can call them Jay and you can call them terrorists till you're blue in the face, but finally you will end up trying to keep them out as you keep yourself in – by building a wall.

Let me tell you something that Callaghan told me about the wall that now snakes across the *Promised Land.* It is not a "fence," it is not a "barrier," it is – as in Berlin – a "wall."

The Israelis and the Palestinians, as a consequence of that wall, are inextricably bound together: if you fuck a dog, it isn't just the dog who howls in pained amazement.

The first casualty of war is not the truth. As for the word *terrorist,* flacks and hacks have done what Ed Sullivan did for the word *wonderful* – they have trivialized it and robbed it of meaning.

The first casualty of war is language.

A theological point.

There's nothing unusual about what I have said about the Son. I grew up taking the idea of the mystery of the Trinity – the idea – for granted: three Persons in One God. Jesus is the Son but He is not the alter ego of the Father. He is at One with and in the Father, just as the Holy Spirit is not a dialectical expression emanating out of the Father and Son. In my more jocular moments, I think of God as being able to chew gum, dance and spin a plate on His nose at the same time. The Son, as it is often said, sits at the Right Hand of God. The angels whom I deplore, those *sinister* angels of the kind who were sent to Sodom, sit at the Left Hand of God.

This brings me to "Himmler's Law."

The originating text is in the Bible: the Sodomites, every last one of them, down to the last little nub of a foetus in the womb, were fried, sizzled, exterminated. Not for sinning. For *being*! Call it what you will, but to me that's genocide, a holocaust.

As for Lot and the angels who visit him, the passage reads – "I have two daughters which have not known man; let me, *I pray you* {italics mine}, bring them out unto you, and do ye to them *as is good in your eyes.*"

And then there's the matter of incest. Lot's daughters drug their father with wine and then bed down with him. "And it came to pass on the morrow, that the firstborn said unto the younger, 'Behold, I lay yesternight with my father; let us make him drink wine this night also; and go thou in, and lie with him, that we may preserve the seed of our father.'" Thus both daughters became pregnant by their father.

This is a dreadful story.

Lot, blotto, two nights in a row, mounts his own daughters. A horny numbskull who ends up with two sons who are called Moab and Ben-ammi. But God did not send angels to assassinate Lot and his daughters, those dreary incestuous scumballs. No, He gave them land!

I had not known how awful this incest story is until I actually read it. Your man Hogg, like most people, had in his youth been given a gloss on stories such as these, had been told that stories such as these contained truths by which we should try to live.

I'm a storyteller. You're a storyteller.

Let us read what is on the page.

Let's get the words right and tell the story.

A last word on the metaphorical and the analogical.

I do not have, as you say, a "worshipful fixation" on John the gospeller. I was speaking of the habit of his metaphorical mind. Look at how he has abetted the endless lunacy of evangelicals. I share none of John's apocalyptic visions and I certainly do not share in the evangelical vision of the conversion of the Jews as a prelude to a final Christian rapture. (Don't you find it ironic that nearly all Zionists welcome the financial and political support of those philo-Semite evangelicals, like the Rev. Hagee of the huge Cornerstone Church in Texas, who pray each day for the total disappearance, through conversion, of *every* believing Jew. If that isn't anti-Semitism lifted to the level of bubblegum metaphysics, I don't know what is. This same Texas nutball recently proclaimed that it is sacrilegious, a sin, for a woman to cry "Oh God" in the midst of her carnal pleasure. This is insane. A denial of what is natural to a human. Where is the sane Mr. Hogg when women need him? He's right here beside the trough, snout at the ready).

As for "The Gift of Tongue" I don't want to drive you totally crazy but:

Communion. The Eucharist. Transubstantiation.

When the priest puts the wafer in the mouth of each communicant, the priest says, "This is the Blood that was shed for you; this is the Body; eat this in remembrance that Christ died for you."

Some communicants experience nothing except a warm feeling: it's just unleavened bread to them.

But to the real believer in The Real Presence, he is eating the sacrificed flesh, the skin and bones.

The wine and bread are not symbolic or emblematic of the body and blood.

They *are*.

One.

That's when the recipient becomes one with the One.

It's not that I practise a belief in this God, or ever go to communion, although Callaghan did at his father's funeral and his son's wedding, twice in the last forty-five years.

My point is, this is a habit of mind, an analogical way of seeing the world. (The inability to experience our lives in this way is what T.S. Eliot meant when he wrote about *a dissociation of sensibility*, a fracturing of our capacity to see things sacramentally that he says took place sometime post-Donne, in the 17th century.)

As for other matters at hand.

Tonguing. And such gifts.

Purity, defilement, and my *amours*.

> *Hogg lay on a shelf*
> *of stone in the valley*
>
> *of Kidron. it was*
> *the dead of night.*
>
> *his neighbours, scattered*
> *among the weeds of*

Olivet Hill, were common
headstones, their bones

the calligraphy of a final
hour. but he and his

woman were naked and
ignored the language

of moss along the bone,
and all grief, calumny,

rage, fell from his eyes
when she knelt and gave him

the gift of tongue. so, too,
the moon swallowed

the sun. his cry named
her and in reply

they heard the muezzin
in his minaret,

that stone shaft into
the mouth of god.

Let's get to what you call the "blasphemy" in my experience,
the defilement in my work that you believe is so removed from
your principles. You recoil from such defilement in your own
poems; in fact, you recoil from any possibility of intimacy – and
intimacy is the key word – with "the uncontrollable mystery on
the bestial floor."

It is a mystery because it is uncontrollable; it is in a mansion but on the floor; it is bestial because, like it or not

...Love has pitched his mansion in
The place of excrement.

—William Butler Yeats

There is sex in your work, and a hothouse sensuality, but little intimacy.

A fish goddess, yes, a snake goddess, yes, a chaste flower, yes...at times you are the Georgia O'Keefe of verse.

Great vulvanating flowers that bees, those burly truck drivers of the sky, drop in on...bzzzz bzzzz...do a dainty-foot dance in...bzzzz...and depart from.

A fribulation of the legs.

Pouch bags filled.

Unsullied by intimacy.

Before going on, let me trust in our friendship and be invasively intimate, oh lusty man that you are. You indeed write about sex, but when you do it reminds me that you can't get over your hateful mother who told you, after your brother died, that she wanted you should have died in his stead. "That cunt," you named her, just after she died, just after she had cut you out of her will. Money was not the issue. She wanted it clear. She had cut you out of her heart. "Fuck her," you said.

Whenever you and I talk about women face to face, we begin my talking about fucking and you end up like James Cagney in *White Heat*, calling, "Mother, Mother..."

And then, rather than freeing yourself by forgiving her, you go off on your own to fish in the inky waters of your brainpan. You try to hook one of the "brides of the stream," unsullied in her diaphanous gown, free from defilement, free from the grave.

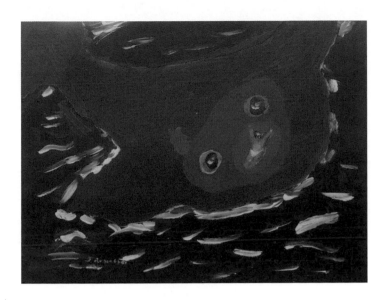

Ah yes, the grave! Why not look at this as Andrew Marvell did? For Marvell, deeply in love with his coy mistress, the place of defilement was the cunt of the grave.

He, as lover, reached down into the land of vermin and hauled his mistress by the living flesh out of that grave where they "tore" their "Pleasures with rough strife / Through the Iron gates of life."

That was pretty daring.

But more daring, Baudelaire jumped right into the grave in *Fleurs du mal*:

> *Alors, ô ma beauté! Dites à la vermine*
> *Qui vous mangera de baisers,*
> *Que j'ai gardé la forme et l'essence divine*
> *Des mes amours decomposes!*

Baudelaire, rather than recoil from corruption, merged eroticism with corruption, so that blasphemy and defilement served to enlarge *la forme et l'essence divine...*

If this seems too Catholic, I will put it in rabbinical terms.

In the Torah, we read that as the Hebrews went out of Egypt, God called: "I am the Lord they God who took you out of Egypt," much as Marvell took his coy mistress out of the grave.

We are told that God's voice was heard in all corners of the earth. There was no echo. Not even in Egypt, that place of defilement. We are to understand, therefore, that God took the Hebrews out of Egypt, not to separate the Light from the Night, but to establish a world in which there would be no barrier against which His voice could rebound. It was to be a world of Oneness in which the liberated, passing through "the Iron Gates of Life," were not just the agents of their own redemption, but the redemption of Egypt – that is, the Hebrews, as they escaped the grave (Egypt) learned that their liberation entailed an embrace of the grave (Egypt, defilement, the cunt).

By liberating and redeeming themselves – they liberated and redeemed the Egyptians.

Or, as that roadside Irish philosopher queen, Crazy Jane, put it to Mr. Yeats's good Bishop – the mansion of love and the place of excrement are not only by nature side-by-side, but nothing can be rent without becoming both sole and whole.

In the rending, in the fucking, is redemption.

I would argue, analogically, that the sexual act in all its coarse sometimes ridiculous energy approaches liberation through intimacy and as such, it is a *tikkun*, a gift. And just as Hogg's woman gives him the gift of tongue (the pentecostal Word, since she is his muse woman), so too, the holy man, crying out from the minaret, the erect stone phallus, thrusts his word into the mouth of the Word, God.

There is no echo.

All are redeemed

If this is blasphemy, so be it, *mon frère, mon semblable*, but it is no more a blasphemy than the Talmudic story of Lilith, who is her own woman, and as such, is so enticing to God that He has taken her as His lover and He cannot get over her. He refuses to give her up, He exalts Himself, so the rabbis tell us, to this day in her human sexuality. God stains the light every day. Exaltation in defilement. What Jean Genet described as "the Eternal passing by in the form of a Pimp."

Come into the grave. Then rise up, my boy, rise up.

Quit your mother, *she dead and gone, Mr. Bones.*

Hogg, the subversive, is in God's image.

God, as Lover, is Hogg's man.

Fondly,
Jim

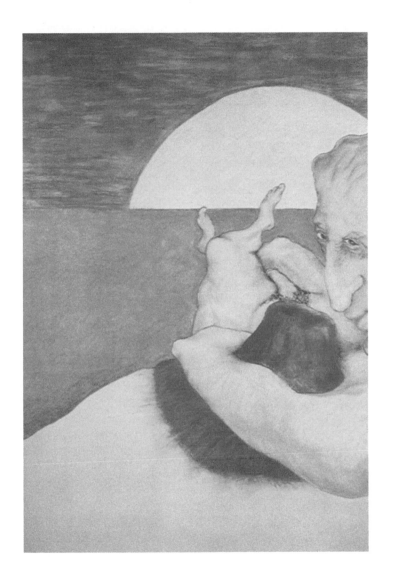

November 12
Mr. James (Jim) Hogg
69 Ophidian Crescent
Mimico, Ontario

Dear Mr. Hogg,

I am sure Mr. Callaghan, given your philosophical digressions down the secular yellow brick road past fields of "tulips," meant no special harshness in calling you "a priggish little prick." Mr. Hogg – Jim, may I call you Jim? – you may prefer to "tiptoe through the tulips," but who under forty can remember that anorexic tinselled American comedian Tiny Tim and his falseto voice as he sang "Tiptoe. . . " etc." in a voice so shrill it could ruffle the plumage of the Angel of Death? There is far too much tulip in your vision. I prefer to tiptoe through the fields of the Destroying Angel.

Today, however, I find myself in an effervescent mood. I owe this effervescence solely to the predacious feline race. During the course of renovations to my residence, workmen laying down some flooring discovered a desiccated bird and a shrivelled rodent under the couch. I suspect Golda (no, not named after the illustrious Golda Meir), but a goddess with striking golden eyes, a quintessence of felinity. My cat did it. I admire ingenuity, whether it is in the crafting of poetry or in the adroit rhythms of mousing or regrettably, bird killing. Cats revere the Stoma precept: EAT or be EATEN.

If we are to engage in philosophical musing via German philosophy, then let us get off on the correct hoof and consider Nietzsche. I appreciate this great philosopher's concept of Dionysian transcendence. Who could fault his striving for the paradigm of a flawless commonwealth selflessly serving the needs of greater humanity? And in fairness to Nietzsche, it must be emphatically stated that his belief in a superman was corrupted by his sister and her husband, both of whom were rabid Jew-haters. It is accepted by Nietzsche scholars that after his death, his sister Elizabeth tampered with his writings to accommodate European fascism. This tampering was greatly enhanced by the Christian Judaeophobia of Nietzsche's admirer, that musical genius of Aryan mythology, Richard Wagner, who not only admired Jewish composers like Mendelssohn and Halévy but befriended the Jewish choirmaster, Heinrich Porges, who went on to receive a life pension from King Ludwig II of Bavaria. Wagner's anti-Semitism leapt over the moon. In a tract published in 1850 in the *Neue Zeitschrift fir Musik*, he ranted, "Jewish music is bereft of all expression, characterized by coldness and indifference, triviality and nonsense." This utterance, from a man who had affairs with a Jewish woman, the singer Giulia Grisi.

You can see, Jim, why I reach for my Uzi when you touch on German philosophy. The Holocaust still resonates with me, and I can't waft it away like so much bog vapour. Jim, you are too fetishized, fettered in your fascination with Heidegger's theoretics. You astound me with your persistent fondling of the silver-tasselled fringes of Teutonic epistemological nihilism.

·HEAT·

You at least concede "that Heidegger with all his talk about Being – the talk that talks to itself of itself – tied himself openly and determinedly to the tyranny of despotic nationalism, to the idea of blood destiny, to Hitler and to the Nazi Party."

Fair enough, you used your cognitive power to unconceal the man's culpability, his fling with German fascism. Sure, "*he dead and gone, Mr. Bones,*" but I hope you have not infected Mr. Callaghan with your eagerness to pick through Heidegger's "brainpan," just as you're all too eager to learn from Ezra Pound's "great gifts – his lucid line, his musical dexterity" – so that you might "turn those gifts against the fascist ideas he espoused; against all levels of State and Party thuggery in our time."

I won't butt heads with you on the above. I know that you mean well with your balanced view of Pound, acknowledging his racist venom against Jews while applauding his contribution to the Modernist movement in poetry. Okay. I've made my Pound point. We'll let it slither past. Suffice to say, I wholeheartedly find myself in agreement with you as you go about "singing a little light into the darkness," but unlike Hannah Arendt, I will not entertain "the possibility of forgiveness."

Regarding Hannah Arendt forgiving Heidegger for his adulation of Hitler, there is only one possible answer: she had been Heidegger's mistress, an academic under his tutelage and influence on German philosophy, back when he was a rising star at the University of Marburg in the early '20s. As an eighteen-year-old she was smitten with her brilliant Martin, and relished the role of the "other woman." Love as a disease can intoxicate. Yet, what I find mystifying is this: one would think that after the Holocaust she would have broken off contact with this apologist for fascism. Why would she try to promote his unfinished manuscript, *Sein und Zeit*, which heavily impacted on 20th-century philosophy – influencing hermeneutics, deconstructionist theory and Existentialism? Yes, the mysterium works in mysterious ways. So does the Stoma in its swallowing of the likes of Heidegger, Hitler, Pound, and yes, eventually, you and me. We will dissolve in the cosmic acid in that Maw of Maws.

I delight in knowing that you have finally come to realize the transcendent ingurgitating power of the Stoma. My favourite metaphor of the Stoma principle is that of a six-hundred-pound Amazonian catfish having its innards devoured by cannibal minnows that the big dumb bewhiskered critter mindlessly lunched upon in the murky depths of that fabulous river, which is one vast moving, eating machine. Why is it that I feel my enemies want to eat my flesh, grind my bones to make their wafers and drink my blood for an orgasmic communion? I have always had to be in a defensive mode against these cannibals, for, as you said: "Just because I am paranoid, doesn't mean they're not trying to get me."

Jim, your glittery vestment is fashioned by forgiveness. I prefer to wear a different outfit, one interwoven with guilt and a loathing for humankind.

Was Mr. Callaghan "delusional" when he raised the matter of Palestinian rights with Prime Minister Golda Meir, when she looked him in the eye and said the Palestinians would be "forgotten in twenty years?"

Mr. Callaghan was prophetically thirty years or more ahead of his time, and the situation has got worse. You mention the present Berlin-styled wall that snakes "across the Promised Land," built to keep Islamic suicide bombers out and protect Israelis, and in doing so, you say, Israel has built its own self-imposed ghetto: the us-against-them mindset is firmly embedded in the psychic mortar of the wall. Mr. Callaghan has imparted to you that "The Israelis and the Palestinians, as a consequence of that wall, are inextricably bound together: if you fuck a dog it isn't just the dog who howls in pained amazement." I take great exception to this debasing of a hapless mutt, as I am more enamoured of dogs than of humankind.

You say, "The first casualty of war is language," because you object to the current overuse of the word *terrorist*, suggesting that the media "flacks and hacks" have puffed the word up just as "Ed Sullivan did for the word *wonderful*...they have trivialized it and robbed it of its meaning." And I suppose it's *wonderfully* true that George Washington would have been regarded as a terrorist by the British, the Irish insurrectionists fighting for an independent Ireland would have been viewed as terrorists, and the British occupying what was then Palestine would have certainly labelled Zionists – the Sinn Féin of the Hebrew Nation – as terrorists of the first order. We are agreed. So goes the bouncing ball on the screen of history.

Given the bounce, let's get to "the matter of a theological point" – your way of reconciling your secular life with your randy theology? You continue to go a hoof afar in your confessional ways, in your quotidian cravings. Let's start with the Trinity.

I plead secular ignorance on the subject of "three persons in One God." It's not my usual turf. However, I find your deconstruction of God offensive. By inferring that He can "dance and spin a plate on His Nose at the same time," you have turned God into a type of clowning, gum-chewing seal! For this transgression alone, I would have you cast into a holding cell in Purgatory; I would have you wear a hair shirt while walking your Stations. You are outrageous. Not only do you have the Creator spinning a plate on His infinite nose, you have the *chutzpah* to dare to advise on the seating arrangement in Heaven, having the "Son seated at the Right Hand of God," and the angels you deplore "seated at the Left Hand of God," who sits plunked down in the middle on His burnished throne. I won't ask where the Hebrew Patriarchs sit. Surely, Heaven isn't an exclusive club for gentiles only? I find your phrase "sinister angels" puzzling. Angels are asexual messengers.

These extraterrestrial messengers came to warn Lot of what was in store for the young men of Sodom if they continued their profligate ways. Please realize that those angels would have been raped if Lot hadn't stopped the rutting pack of sinners in their tracks. I ask you to lighten up. You are far too fixated on the tribal morality of the beardy patriarchs. By the way, how did you come by the news that Abraham's beard was infested with lice? Would you say the same thing about Jesus, and his Jewish Apostles? (Well, now that I think about it, you just might.) I definitely think you should cut back on your poetic hypertext with its hyperbolic leaps of logic.

It's bad enough impugning Abraham's beard, but to bring your designated "Himmler's Law" into the picture is one hell of an analogous leap to the nine moons orbiting Saturn. At least nobody can argue that you're politically correct when you refer to the fiery extermination of the Sodomites by a Hebrew God's vengeful wrath, for as you put it, even the innocent down to the last little nub of a foetus yet to be born, "were fried, sizzled, exterminated. Not for sinning. For *being*! Call it what you will, but to me that's genocide, a holocaust."

Fair comment. The Hebrew God got carried away. He wasn't too pleased with the sinful goings on in Sodom city to start with, but what particularly got His sacrificial goat was that the horny gay lads of Sodom had impure designs on his beardless messengers. Now I believe that angels are hermaphroditic, and quite possibly, according to some Bible scholars, neutered. And so, Lot's offer of his daughters to those downy messengers would have gone nowhere. And then, there's this business of the cave, which has rattled you: *incest.* You have the two daughters conspiring to have some experiential sex with their bearded dad, and so you quote a prurient dollop of evidential scripture from Genesis: *The firstborn said unto the younger, 'Our father is old, and there is not a man in the earth to come in unto us after the manner of all the earth; come, let us make our father drink wine, and we will lie with him, that we may preserve seed of our father.' And they made their father drink wine that night: and the firstborn went in and lay with her father; and he perceived not when she lay down, nor when she arose. And it came to pass on the morrow, that the firstborn said unto the younger, 'Behold I lay yesternight with my father; let us make him drink wine this night also; and go thou in, and lie with him, that we may preserve seed of our father.' And they made their father drink wine that night also; and the younger arose, and lay with him; and he perceived not when she lay down, nor when she arose. Thus were both the daughters of Lot with child by their father.*

The above shocks you. "A dreadful story," yes, but let me assure you that many a case worker can offer much more disturbing files, stories that would grow hair on a billiard ball. You are horrified that Lot "blotto, out of his mind on drink, two nights in a row, mounts his own daughters," and "ends up with two sons who are called Moab and Ben-ammi." I would be willing to bet you dollars to doughnuts that incest is more common than you think in our society: how many women seek a shrink years after having been sexually assaulted by their dads, when they were most vulnerable as children?

Why then go to some desert cave and heap abuse on a drunken old hairy sot? Sure, Lot's wife didn't deserve to end up as "a salt lick for camels." She was, however, warned by those downy messengers not to turn around and witness the barbequing of Sodom. She did just that, and presto, became a salty number. Nasty retribution, but having said that, I wish you would find a different nomenclature for God's vengeful genocide of Sodom's populace, sinners and innocent babes, a genocide of unimaginable magnitude – a term other than "Himmler's Law?"

Let us not forget about that terrible ex-seminarian, Stalin, the Little Father, as he was known by his own loving people... let us not forget his murderous reign, his man-made famine, the millions of dead peasants starved through forced collectivization in Ukraine in the '30s; "Stalin's Law" would do just fine. And why not consider as well Pol Pot, that engineer of agrarian socialism? I appeal to you – give "Pol Pot's Law" a chance – give this mastermind of the Cambodian Holocaust a contemporaneous kick at the genocidal can? Why only "Himmler's Law?"

You are like a man riven by swamp fever. Why are you so glued to incest? What's most interesting in the Good Book is its bare-ass honesty in the chronicling of ancient human history in the Middle East, the baring of all...hair, wens, zits, incest, fratricide, matricide, patricide, infanticide, anger, jealously, bisexuality, heterosexuality, homosexuality, mythomania, hypocrisy, war and violence, human sacrifice, animal offerings, betrayal, binge sex, copious imbibing, murderous warrior women, frantic gyres, the dancing to flutes and tambourines by stoned Semites in the painted buff, worship of the Golden Calf, and much more – that is, until monotheistic Moses laid his singed tablets and its Ten Commandments on the ten tribes of Israel.

Jim, no matter how many quotes, chapter and verse, you slam-dunk into the loop of my brain, I say, "Give it up or you'll end up in a rubber room."

You must take care. You'll never fit into Christ's sandals. By your own admission, it takes "the real believer in the Real Presence." You'll always be famished for the tasty Jesus Loaf, for the full gustatory presence of the Son of God. I feel pity for you and am reminded of the first two lines of Emily Dickinson's poem, "God Gave a Loaf to Every Bird."

God gave a loaf to every bird,
But just a crumb to me;

You are only worthy of receiving a crumb at the long table of The Last Supper. The big loaves go to the Faithful, who are regular church attendees. I must digress here and inject a note of levity; take a breather, we're getting somewhat theologically heavy.

I think your "habit of mind" has been awash with too much runaway Dionysian prurience. Instead of passive recollection, quietude and a union of the soul with God, you have chosen to blasphemously revise several sacred Judeo-driven Christian precepts, while giving offence to their beardy Abrahamic roots! I am embarrassed for your sake! Your thoughts should be calmer, more quietly reflective and focused on God's white light. Can you not follow the example of the great mystic, St. Teresa of Avila (1515–82), her miraculous imaginings of the interiority of her Fourth Mansion and the extreme delight she took fashioning her prayers to the design of her heavenly mansion?

Haven't you complained of your body prison in *Hogg*? I know you realize that the wall exists, that the body steadily decays, and while it lives, it excretes waste, smells of foul wind and halitosis, makes eerie noises in copulating heat, and then like a crazed Banshee, emits an orgasmic screeching – the poor *soul* lies about trying to get a decent night's sleep. Realize it: your spiritual envelope is a wee electrical myna bird longing to leave your body prison. Jim, you have the twisted temerity to visualize the Judeo-Christian God as gay, performing fellatio on a minaret. It leaves me wondering if you have gone barking mad. I will have you know that God is as straight as the CN Tower.

Of course, I call your amative thinking, when it goes off the rails, blasphemy... your dysfunctional intimacy as you move vertiginously in sync with "the uncontrollable mystery on the bestial floor." My preferred floor, however, is the unspoiled natural world; not a vulnerable church graveyard exposed to the practices of an erotophilic individual with an overactive sexual economy. I steer away from graveyards, preferring instead the company of buzzing bees – working themselves to death in a frenzied dance of cross-pollination, so that you and I can be sure grapes will be there for the harvest, so we can drink palatable wine. This is my kind, my form, of intimacy. I say, "*Vive la différence!*" Perhaps

> *...Love has pitched his mansion*
> *In the place of excrement*

but I say: "No, thank you." The thought of shit linked with romance may be a mystery to you , but it is less of a mystery for me. I am too much the puritan to associate the two, and no, I don't care for such mystery. How dare you say there is no intimacy in my work? You forget the intimacy of my marine sonnets, my fondling the fish in my boat after I have secured my "catch of the day," usually ling cod, my exploring, call it foreplay – fondling their breathing bodies, their quivering fins – in full arousal, their dark pleading eyes fixed on me moments before I dispatch the lot with my "priest," as an angler's club is called in my part of the world – and you say there is sex, but no intimacy in my poetry? What codswallop! Think of the fresh intimacy and the consummation when I finally get to eat the finny ones. What could be more intimate than that? You do, however, honour me by admitting there is sex in my work, and admire its "luxurious hot house sensuality," but alas, no intimacy! Nevertheless, I accept praise from intelligent life on earth, starting with your praise of my marine and snaky musings, and "a classic flower," by which, I take it, you mean a bee-induced *la petite mort*, regarding my chanting "Bumblebee Dithyramb" – but am I "at times...the Georgia O'Keefe of verse?"

On still another matter: your revelation that I am obsessed about fucking comes as a complete surprise. You say, whenever Callaghan and I talk about women face to face, we end up talking about fucking and I end up like James Cagney in *White Heat*, calling, "Mother, Mother…" My hating my hateful mother is one thing, Cagney crying out for the mother he loves in that compelling movie, is quite another. But what does this have to do with the art of fucking?

Have you lost control of your senses in suggesting that I bite through the "umbilical cord" and go on my own to "fish in the inky lake waters of my brainpan?" I appreciate the metaphor cobbled together from my musings – but the rest of your request, urging me to "free myself from the grave," is gobsmack refused: I shall never forgive my mother for leaving me out of her will. She was a piece of crap!

I hope you don't confuse our Mr. Callaghan by bending his ear with your metaphysical gymnastics. It may distract him from betting on a winning nag, racing to the finish line, as seen on a monitor in some palatial betting den.

"Ah yes, the grave." This time I am relieved to know I am not crawling out of my sainted mother's grave. Fast forward to Andrew Marvell, "deeply in love with his coy Mistress." You have Marvell reach into the "cunt" of the grave, "where Worms shall try that long preserved Virginity, that fine and private place." The bard's words resonate in my mind. But not to be bested by Marvell, you become exceedingly descriptive, making sure I get full impact of your message: "He, as lover, reached down into the land of vermin and hauled his mistress by the living flesh out of that grave…" Scary stuff. Not satisfied to end what any sensible being would consider a necrophilic tendency, you continue your fascination with "corruption, merged eroticism with corruption," bringing the Immortal Baudelaire into the grim picture by having him jump into the grave, where, in

the great bard's words: *Des mes amours decomposes*! This is like a nightmare when one bolts up to find oneself in a casket covered in worms. What in blazes does love have to do with decomposition? Love is for the living, and that can be something akin to smoking divine opium: habit-forming.

You appear to agree with Baudelaire, that blasphemy and defilement only enlarge *la forme et l'essence divine*… It all escapes me. Baudelaire seemed inspired by decomposition and you only have to read Roy Campbell's excellent translation of "The Carcase," the same poem you quoted in the original from *Les Fleurs du mal*, to realize the extent of Baudelaire's fascination with one particular decomposing carcass, which he finds to be "a poison-sweating mass," that balloons "with evil gas," and "on this putrescence," the sun manages to blaze the unmentionable oozing rot with gold.

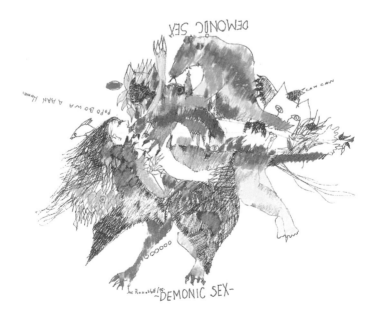

Jim, look again into the grave, observe flies and "larvae poured in legions far and wide." In this poem, Baudelaire and a friend happen to have come upon a rotting animal with "liquescent jelly" running over "rags of hide." It's hard to believe that this is all happening on an idyllic sunny day.

I think that you have mistaken a rotting carcass the poet happened upon with the open grave that he is alleged to have jumped in. I will have to consult with Mr. Callaghan on this matter, retired professor that he is. I am sure he will be enthused enough to steer me to the right gravesite:

> *Then tell the vermin as it takes its pleasance*
> *And feasts with kisses on that face of yours,*
> *I've kept intact in form and godlike essence*
> *Our decomposed amours!*

I rather like your analogy, strained as it is, and explained to me in "rabbinical terms," where you compare the ancient Hebrews escaping from Egyptian bondage and "defilement" to Marvell taking his coy mistress out of the grave. That "God's echo can find no barrier to echo back to Him" is mythically charged and in keeping with His Oneness, yet this is a far cry from the miniscule oneness of Marvell fancying a woman who has rebuffed his advances and his desire to take her romping through "the iron gates of life." I suspect she rejected his advances completely and rescuing her from the grave was merely a decorative post-delusional fantasy. Marvell, like yourself, is simply a victim in that long agglutinated train of Tough Love:

> *Let us roll all our strength, and all*
> *Our sweetness, up into one ball;*
> *And tear our pleasures with rough strife*
> *Thorough the iron gates of life.*

Am I being silly in asking whether one can find redemption, redemption for yourself, through fucking? I find this repugnant. Is this a form of intimacy and, if it is, needn't we revise the Ten Commandments? Your Gift of Tongue has strayed into a bawdy house where tongues become feral extensions of barnyard urges. I am tempted to say you need Pentecostal Pete to cast out the three hundred devils residing in you.

The apostle Paul writes, "He who speaks in tongues edifies himself...I would like every one of you to speak in tongues." You need to send a tongued message to the Maker of the Universe and ask for His Divine Forgiveness for your many blasphemies, too numerous to mention. Jim, let Pete help you seek the White Light. It may mean grasping a few venomous snakes while you shout for redemption, seeking to edify yourself. You can follow the example of holy rollers who challenge the fates by tempting Satan, embodied in that serpent. If any member is bitten and perishes, it's because he or she has sinned. Your juxtapositions and analogies are jarring. Stay clear of incest, as revealed in Baudelaire's romantic attraction to his sister, in his "L'invitation au voyage." And be damned with Lot and his daughter and their alleged incestuous relations with their bearded dad.

Jim, I won't bullshit you, being a high school dropout, I don't know what to make of your comments on Baudelaire's "blasphemy and defilement" that "enlarge *la forme et l'essence divine*." I will pass on that; suffice it to say: there is a limit to poetic licence when it comes to the grave and merging "eroticism and corruption." I am tempted to suggest that Baudelaire, Marvell, and possibly Poe, plus a confluence of early 17th-century metaphysical poets, may have brought a Heavy Metal influence to bear on your poetic vision with their conjoined blasphemies.

In a deeper sense, you have your hard-core fixations which, to my way of thinking, are idolatrous, idols of those bipolar bards who'd jump into the grave to seize the mortal remains of women they have fancied. You have made idols of Jesus, Mary, virgins, whores, idols of the Abrahamic line from the Hebrew patriarchs. You have unfairly maligned them. My point? They are all idols, so it matters little if it is the Virgin Mary you are revering, or some woman pleasuring you among the patriarchal crypts in a church graveyard, or a Bedouin woman indulging your needs in a desert tent under the starry sky. The point is that you worship idols, plain and simple – Queen of Heaven, Crazy Jane, your Queen of the Leningrad Canals, or any contemporaneous chick, shapely enough to awe you and seduce you. I am tempted to ask if they were immaculately virginal before you offered them the trouser worm.

Is Lilith your latest crush? I think God was asking for trouble when He made Eve out of Adam's rib, having earlier fashioned Lilith. Depending on what branch of Semitic lore one values in the myth of Lilith, she has become a feminist icon – Adam's ignored first wife, created at the same time, yet a woman scorned by certain Hebrew and Christian scribes, typecast as an evil demon. The 13th-century Rabbi Isaac ben Jacob ha-Kohen expostulates in his writings that Lilith left Adam, refusing to be subservient to Adam and ignoring his plea to return to the Garden of Eden after she made whoopee with the archangel Samuel. In any case, she took a bad rap, and you're not helping matters by suggesting she conducted an affair with God "who refuses to give her up."

You have unnamed rabbinical sources declare that, because of God's indiscretion with Lilith, humankind faces "human pain and defilement. God stains the light every day. Exaltation in defilement." What passage from what obscure sacred text did this bouncing revelation issue from? Could it be that you read some exegesis from the Aramaic in some Gnostic text? You sure know how to blaspheme, as though you were turning a wheel of blasphemies in lieu of a prayer wheel.

I would like to end this letter by thanking you for your advice in going for closure over the matter of my mother's betrayal. I hear you calling out to me from the grave I have dug. "Quit your mother, she dead and gone, Mr. Bones." Yes, my mother is finally dead. Dead. Write to me, Jim. Always delighted to receive a missive from you, however punishing.

Warmest regards,
JR

PS: I hope I've not crossed the line with my petulance. Apologies given in advance.

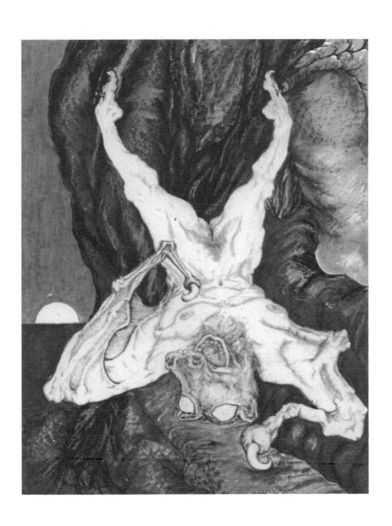

August 12

Dear Joe, my old friend.
It's Callaghan here:

I have shut Gatemouth Hogg down.

Admittedly, he has a talent, a talent for disputation and bad-
inage, but enough is enough – too much *caca*demic learning. In
each of his letters, he's gone on and on and on…about himself,
nailed by the feet (he is, at best, Peter not Jesus) to his own cross
– on and on about who *he* thinks I am, intending to correct who
you think I am. "Suh," I say, "there's been altogether too much
Hogg, too much hogwash about Hogg."

How I've got stuck with this would-be seminarian walking
around in my shoes is beyond me.

His hectoring about the Eucharist, sex, shit, and sin tells
me he really should spend some more time (not less) with
Doctor Ded and Medusa among her Moochers (and take you
with him, away from your metaphorical garden of flowering
pudenda).

His impertinence, his appropriation of my intentions and
aspirations in his letters has been astounding. If I thought for a
second that I was both Sartrean and Lacanian, I'd slit my wrists.

As for Heidegger, I haven't read him in years. Constipated
prose, which is what he shared with that other Kraut, Luther. It
is a fact, Luther would sit all day on the shitter, a one-holer,
straining at stool while dreaming of bowel-release (grace) and
absolute authority, straining for a cleansing. A despotic God
that he saw through the half-moon in the door, call it Jehovah,
call it Being…'tis to me all the same puritan rejection of the
flesh. Grace, I repeat, came to Luther like a pill, like a laxative,
as a cleansing, an enema. Heidegger hitched himself to Hitler
who was going to cleanse the blood… *Aargh.*

Appalling lunatics, but still, I don't understand your near-*dictat* that no one should read Heidegger with serious interest because he in fact doffed his cap and did a deep bow to Hitler.

Gertrude Stein wrote speeches for Marshall Pétain. Should I not read her? Should I not read Knut Hamsun, who became a Nazi, saying, "Hitler has spoken to my heart" and who, with all his heart, became a supporter of Quisling and betrayed his country, Norway? Should it matter to me that Thomas Mann, in 1955, said, "The stigma of his {Hamsun's} politics will be one day separated from his writing, which I regard very highly"? Should it matter to me that Isaac Bashevis Singer said that "the whole modern School of Literature in the 20th century stems from Hamsun's novel, *Hunger*" (1890)?

Even more to the point: – the greatest French novelist of the 20th century was (and is) Céline, who hung out in Vichy and reviled and excoriated the Jews, especially in his two rants just before the war: "…the pretty puss of the average kike…Those spying eyes, lyingly pale…that uptight smile…those livestock lips" – on and on he goes. Yet all the while his writing – his tone, his style – had enormous influence on Gide, Genet, Henry Miller, Vonnegut, Mailer, Burroughs, LeRoi Jones, Leon Rooke (who has Heidegger as a tall-tale "comic" figure in a story about measuring Heidegger's cranium), and Philip Roth, who said, "To tell you the truth, in France, my Proust is Céline. There's a very great writer. Even if his anti-Semitism made him an abject, intolerable person. To read him I have to suspend my Jewish conscience, but I do it, because his anti-Semitism isn't at the heart of his books, even *Castle to Castle*. Céline is a great liberator. I feel called by his voice."

Liberation.

The call of the voice…turn to the call of another voice, other hatreds: your mother.

A woman, by your own account, who deserved to be hated if only because of the fact she treated you, her most vulnerable son, so hatefully.

Because of her, Hogg says that when you write about sex, there is no intimacy to that sex. (I can't tell you how repulsive your fondling and stroking of a fish in the urgency and flop of dying is to me.)

No intimacy! All flowers and *bombinating* bumblebees (to steal a word from Layton's great brag of a love poem to Aviva), so Hogg says.

Well, yes, but no, good sir.

Years ago you wrote a fine prose piece, "The Lake." It is to be read, I believe like Blake's "The Rose," at several levels: the direct matter of a dangerous dive deep into the unknown waters of a black lake; or a dangerous dive into the unknown waters of your imagination seeking illumination in the darkest deep of blackness; or – and this is the reading I favour – the dangerous dive the lover makes into the darkest waters of the cunt (see Henry Miller's "metaphysics of fuck" in *The Tropic of Capricorn*), the lover risking who he *is* in what can only be called – and this may be embarrassing to your mendacious sense of yourself – an act of deeply felt, penetrating intimacy.

I leave you on that note, good sir, as I leave Hogg, who has been too much with us.

Your old pal,
Barry

"ANGELS IN FUR"

- J. Rosenblatt - 2009 -

September 24,

Dear Barry,

Before you close Gatemouth Hogg down, there is a matter I want to clear up in my final epistle to you.

I will agree that, in part, there is a lack of intimacy in my writings. That is, there is a lack of *human intimacy* regarding my muse. I confess there is far too much distance from my subject matter. But please take into consideration that my muse is powered by fanciful creatures, a private bestiary, an exotic zoo or aquarium so to speak, rampant with the voluptuous brides of Neptune (see my volume of marine sonnets, *Tentacled Mother*). Having said that, well, it's true, I rarely rap about people in my poetry. The intimacy, if there is such a critter, lies in the domain of my memoirs, which you edited and saw to publication in 1974, *Escape from the Glue Factory*, my childhood memoirs of growing up in Toronto in the '40s. I could be confusing nearness with intimacy, as in a piece in that volume, "The Lake," but I believe nearness and intimacy are interchangeable. How much more intimate can I get than to send my imagination to plunge into the freezing inky depths of an archetypal northern lake, to seek the light, and in my quest, have passersby of deep lake trout for company? Wouldn't you allow that intimacy reigned as I pressed against those fish? Well, yes, you would, you have said so. And so it must be true, Hogg be jiggered.

You, more than other creative writers, from Day One praised my bee poems, as you continue to do, as you just did in your last missive to me referring to "all flowers and *bombinating* bumblebees." I, too, as I inch toward death, shall steal that word from Layton's love poem to Aviva and think of myself as bombinating.

Regarding Henry Miller and his "metaphysics of fuck," what's to say? Perhaps you're right in stating that this "act of deep penetrating intimacy" may be "embarrassing" to my "mendacious sense." The word "cunt" frightens me. It shatters my puritanical ears and temperament. And finally, this last confession to you, Barry, friend of forty years and more and now my confessor: I prefer being the voyeur, I prefer to observe the honeybee diving deep into the cunts of hollyhocks. I, of course, wouldn't call them cunts, deep throats maybe, but never cunts. By nature, I am not so raw. I will say only this: It was a pleasure carrying on an epistolary discourse with Jim, rat-a-tap-tapping by proxy on your proboscis as a way of embracing some of life's truths (and confusions), yes, a pitter-patter of animated vitalities all under the roof of heaven.

Joe

Poem for a Dying Bumblebee

The thorns know the hour
a dusty tourist strikes the rose —
flowers are not born; they grow
for this traveller in his tiny vestment
who falls on his pollen-laden elbows
in Momma's tabernacle, in October.

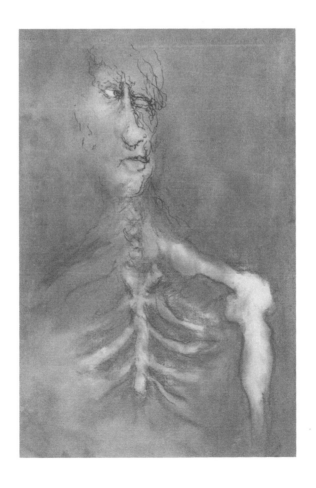

INDEX OF THE ART

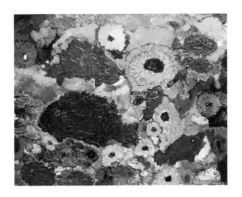

The artworks that appear in this volume
are by Barry Callaghan and Joe Rosenblatt.

Half-title and Title pages artwork by Chris Roberts

Barry Callaghan's photograph by Mark Tearle

Joe Rosenblatt's photograph by Faye C. Smith-Rosenblatt